NEW LEFT REVIEW EDITIONS

Reimut Reiche

NLB

# Sexuality and
# Class Struggle

First published as
*Sexualität und Klassenkamp*
by Verlag Neue Kritik, 1968
© Verlag Neue Kritik, 1968
This edition first published 1970
Translated from the German by Susan Bennett
Preface and Postscript translated by
David Fernbach
© NLB, 1970

NLB, 7 Carlisle Street, W1

Designed by Gerald Cinamon
Typeset in Monotype Ehrhardt
and printed by
Western Printing Services Ltd, Bristol

SBN  902308  40  8

*Author's note*: I would like to thank all the comrades who took part in the seminars on 'Sexuality and Political Power' organized by the Argument Club in West Berlin in 1963 and 1964 and by the SDS – the German Socialist Student Movement – elsewhere, as well as all those who participated in the many meetings and discussions of the AUSS – Independent High-School Students' Action Centre – whose views forced me to think out my own and to write this book.

*Acknowledgement*: Thanks are due to The Hogarth Press for their kind permission to quote from The Standard Edition of the Complete Psychological Works of Sigmund Freud.

# Preface
# to the English Edition

*Sexuality and Class Struggle* was written in West Germany in the winter of 1967–8 at the time of the great Vietnam demonstrations and the first school strikes, before the wave of university occupations began, and between the first police killing of a student (2 June 1967) and the attempted assassination of Rudi Dutschke (Easter 1968). University occupations, experiments in collective child upbringing, the autonomous organization of study and education, instigation of revolts in the superstructure and actions to expose 'consumer terrorism' – all of which formed the main period of 'self-organization' – had not yet been crystallized either in our heads or in our practice. This period and its birth-pangs can only be interpreted in retrospect as a first step towards the reconstruction of the revolutionary movement in West Germany. At the time it was no more than a protest movement; this was also true of its temporary leaders and theorists, conscious socialists or highly educated Marxist though they may have been as individuals. We ourselves termed this protest movement the 'anti-authoritarian movement'. The name APO – extra-parliamentary opposition – was given it (and especially its outer periphery) by the bourgeois press; it corresponds neither to our theories at that time, nor to our form of organization, nor – so far – to our political aims. To begin with the movement was highly practical and deeply moral; practical, in so far as it broke sharply with the purely theoretical reflections of university Marxists and the Frankfurt School of critical theory, as also with the clandestine revisionism and paper alliances of the Communist Party; moral, in so far as the movement derived its initial political and emotional force by making people aware of the suppressed promises of bourgeois emancipation. The protest movement was however just as *abstract* in its practical activist concerns as it was historically *necessary*. It was *necessary*, in order to recreate as a general political experience the dimension of a conscious and collective historical process which had been submerged in the most developed and technologically advanced class societies.

Due to fascism and its posthumous effects in the reconstruction period of capitalist democracy, the tradition of the revolutionary workers' movement has nowhere been so lastingly destroyed as in Germany. Our movement was *abstract* as we could find no way of connecting in practice the visible violence of imperialism with the forms of violent social relations within the countries of late capitalism, for the latter were necessarily concealed by morality, law and the rise in standard of living, in a manner which we were impotent to confront. Owing to the historic break in the revolutionary tradition, our hopes of bourgeois emancipation and proletarian revolution, and bourgeois enlightenment and proletarian class consciousness, converged in our political theory and separated in our practice to a greater extent than in the period of open class struggle that preceded fascism.

Compared with these political problems, particular aspects of which are discussed in *Sexuality and Class Struggle*, the book's treatment of sexual theory or psycho-analysis proper is of lesser importance. The work was never conceived as a contribution to sexual theory or psycho-analysis. What nevertheless appears as such in the book is very often the result of my own private observations – with all the subjective distortions which affect intellectual products, all the more when they are concerned with psychological processes. But what gives the book the character of a political document is not my private work. Certainly I *wrote* it myself, but I wrote it in a political situation in which my comrades and I were completely absorbed. The book is a direct result of a political experience that was not unique to me, and of theoretical reflections that were still less only my own.

So this book is, I believe, not really a document of 'anti-authoritarian theory' in the strict sense. I personally am one of the comrades in our movement who developed theoretically and were politically socialized long before the protest movement began, who initiated the movement, became its spokesmen, and, from a certain point on, also its indigenous product. This distinguished us on the one hand from those of our contemporaries who remained 'seminar Marxists' or 'adepts of critical theory', and on the other from those comrades for whom the anti-authoritarian movement played a far more direct and influential role in their own lives and political development. This fact also shows itself at some points in the book (especially, I think, in the treatment of the 'First Commune', which is paternalistically sympathetic rather than directly involved). Today the anti-authoritarian movement is considered as historically terminated and politically superseded. The stereotype reference to it at all meetings and in all papers of our groups is 'the anti-authoritarian period of the movement'. Historically terminated it certainly is, at least in so far as there simply are no more campaigns or revolts of university or school students which bear the distinguishing features of the action and organization of the anti-authoritarian movement; at most these flare up only sporadically and in backward parts of the country. Whether it has really been superseded in the development of our theory, organization and practice is however still questionable.

The protest movement reached a peak in early summer 1968. In summer 1969 for the first time, significant groups came out with the slogans: 'Wipe out the anti-authoritarian trash' and 'Liquidate the anti-authoritarian phase'. During this period the anti-authoritarian movement had at first developed consistently. Then it became increasingly blocked by its own limitations until it finally turned into a farce, and for many also a tragedy. The theoretical conceptions and organizational expressions of this development, in their order of appearance, were: dissolution of the whole movement and its reorganization in 'communes'; self-organization of study through the setting-up of anti-universities; upbringing of children in anti-authoritarian collectives; re-organization of the entire private life of all comrades in 'collective educational processes', creation of a 'counter-milieu' etc.; forcible demolition of the old university and other exemplary repressive institutions (press monopoly, draft offices, war research centres); reorganization of the movement in clandestine terrorist groups; departure to the hashish underground; and resurrection as class-conscious 'Marxist-Leninist' proletarians pledged to the service of the people. Naturally not every group and individual passed through all these stages. However the minority who actually did only epitomized the frantic character which the anti-authoritarian movement indigenously acquired at a specific stage in its development and in which it proceeded to disintegrate.

While *Sexuality and Class Struggle* was criticized in early 1969 for being not consistent *enough* in its anti-authoritarianism, already six months later it was classified as an 'anti-authoritarian aberration'. Both criticisms, made at specific phases, have a true and a false aspect. It is correct that I took up a very nebulous, in part even opportunist position on some issues (child education, monogamy). The second criticism is also correct in so far as the book is not based on any clear class analysis, and the question of the subject of the revolution is answered voluntaristically (viz. the treatment of which class is today combatting capitalism, in Chapter 1). Also, the way in which capitalism affects the organization of instinctual drives was analysed only *vis-à-vis* consumption, and the effect of the production process itself was scarcely mentioned.

However, now that the anti-authoritarian limitations of our movement are 'superseded', the reverse danger has arisen of a rigid recantation of all our revolutionary demands, and the consequent decay of our revolutionary legitimacy. Today many comrades and groups seek quite abstractedly to deny the history of *their* movement, and thereby their own history. This happens in three kinds of way: in a dehumanizing split into theory without practice ('training') and practice without theory (work at the 'base'); in a pragmatic *realpolitik* bordering dangerously on reformism; in a dogmatic return to the Leninist model of organization which, in the *ahistorical* use often made of it among us, becomes an authoritarian and bureaucratic game of strategy, involving 'a student/workers' party without workers'.

Future political battles and our aim of developing class struggle in the Federal Republic certainly demand an increased degree of organizational discipline. In the anti-authoritarian phase of our movement, we 'solved' organizational questions in our characteristic manner of spontaneous voluntarism, by simply failing to distinguish action and organization. We should not now make the reverse errors and 'solve' organizational questions by an abstractly dogmatic and rigid voluntarism, by appropriating the ready-made organizational 'model' of the Bolshevik party. The devastating consequences that this produces where, as with us, the situation is still not one of real class struggle, can be seen most plainly and most painfully in the acute lack of *practical solidarity* which now prevails in the movement. During the anti-authoritarian period a permanent 'emancipation debate' was carried on which was the spontaneously organized expression of our cultural revolutionary programme. This demanded of each single comrade a degree of reflection, openness and readiness to change his whole personality which was often so high that many comrades were broken by the psychological pressure. With the end of the anti-authoritarian 'phase' this emancipation debate dissolved, on the premiss – in itself correct – that the emancipation debate, as we had conducted it, expressed our petty-bourgeois class limitations and the psychologizing of political and class questions that followed from this. However the dissolution of the emancipation debate necessarily led to a destruction of our legitimacy, for *we* did not acquire a class and political identity by suddenly acknowledging ourselves Marxist–Leninists.

Thus the newly flourishing organizational rigidity and authoritarian allegiance of some 'Marxist–Leninists' is only one side, and even a harmless one, of the process through which many comrades hoped to reinforce their class and revolutionary identity. The other side of the same process, much more dangerous for the development of class solidarity and class struggle, is the decay of practical solidarity or, in other words, the collective regression to a petty-bourgeois level of human relations. This regression is a necessary consequence of the mechanistic imitation of the Leninist organizational 'model'. (I am in no way saying that the Leninist party principle is 'repressive' in itself; on the contrary, the Bolshevik party in its time expressed both the tasks *and* the needs of the revolutionary vanguard. Only because of this could it become the party of the proletariat.) This regression is expressed in the manifold *splits* which have no real political explanation and hence scarcely any elucidatory function; in the *tactical manoeuvres* and *deceptions* within the movement, which we so much detested and which were quite new to us; in the *defamation* and, most tragically, in the *isolation* of and damage done to comrades who had earlier found their political and emotional identity 'in the movement'.

The developments just described are only *tendencies* within a necessary process of clarification for our movement. I interpret them in no way as signalling a *decline* of the movement. Nevertheless, in view of these tendencies *Sexuality and Class Struggle* can be said to display a naïve optimism and also a fundamental vagueness, marking both the strength and the intrinsic limits of our movement.

*Reimut Reiche*
*Frankfurt, May 1970*

# Chapter 1
# What has Class Struggle
# to do with Sexuality?

In the period following the collapse of fascism, the socialists and
the rest of the radical opposition in Germany paid very little
attention to the question of sexuality in their political programmes. The emancipation of women was regarded by the
trade unions, the SPD (German Social Democratic Party), and
the other large organizations, as simply a matter of eliminating
discrepancies in the social and legal status of the sexes, and in
many quarters it was felt that even here the demand for absolute
equality need not be too strictly interpreted. In their time, the
political demands which had arisen under the Weimar Republic
(1919–33) for the deletion from the legal code of the para-
graphs on abortion and homosexuality, though essentially
bourgeois-egalitarian, had given the impetus to a very broad
popular front on the issue. Under the Federal Republic, such
demands have been confined to humanistic circles, and have at
best given rise to brief campaigns or petitions to parliament.
There has been nothing comparable to the Sexpol movement
(see p. 14) of the pre-fascist era, located within and on the
fringe of the proletarian organizations. The reason for this lies,
on the one hand, in the far-reaching changes effected in West
Germany on the workers' movement and the socialist movement in general after their defeat under fascism, and their
second defeat in the post-war era of capitalist reconstruction;
and on the other, in the drastic change in the role of sexuality
under the post-fascist regime.

This book grew out of an actual situation: the theoretical
discussions and active political controversy taking place in West
Germany at the present time, in which sexuality, political
struggle and social liberation all play a part. Yet it deals almost
exclusively with one aspect of the question: the change in the
role of sexuality under the cultural dominance of late capitalism.
The reason for this is not an academic desire to limit the field of
study. The methods of ruling human beings under contemporary capitalism have borrowed in so sophisticated a manner

from the sexual revolution that a naïve belief in the self-libera-
ting force of sexuality under such a system is no longer easy.
There have in fact only been two movements within the radical
camp in West Germany which have openly attempted to formulate the problems of sexuality and have combined the aim of
social emancipation with a direct aim to revolutionize sexuality:
the First Commune in West Berlin and the Independent High-
School Students' Action Centre (AUSS). But in practice, their
attempts to revolutionize the sexual attitudes of society and the
sexuality of their own members, or to incorporate the necessity
of such a revolution into a programme of political enlightenment, have so far been a failure. The reasons for this failure lie
on the one hand in the almost insoluble problem of the 'already
formed' sexual character of those they are attempting to revolutionize, and on the other in a self-contradictory conception of
sexuality in their theory of anti-capitalist, anti-authoritarian
struggle. It is mainly for these reasons that I have chosen in this
book to treat the current *political* questions principally from one
angle: sexual oppression in late capitalism, and the economic
and psychological preconditions for defensive action against
such oppression. The other side of the question, the practical
measures to be taken to spread sexual liberation, and the means
by which people can organize themselves to this end, has
remained very sketchy, and at times has had to be left completely
open.

Wilhelm Reich, in the last years before the onset of fascism,
realized that these aims were not compatible with the belief,
common to the S P D and K P D (the German Communist
Party), in party politics and agitation. In both these parties, the
community of membership, leaders and masses as a single
fighting unit was on the wane. The parties could no longer represent the interests of the masses, because they did not understand
them. The S P D and K P D were perpetuating themselves in the
form of ever stronger and ever more authoritarian machines.[1]

From this, Reich drew an at least partially correct conclusion. He built up a movement for Sexual Economy and
Politics – Sexpol – which saw itself as a group within the communist workers' movement. A very large number of youth
groups, medical advisory centres, and teachers' and doctors'
groups belonged to Sexpol; they organized working parties,
evening instruction sessions, and sex education meetings. By

[1] This situation was analysed by Wilhelm Reich under the pseudonym Ernst
Parell in *Was ist Klassenbewusstsein?* ('What is Class Consciousness?'), Verlag für Sexualpolitik, Copenhagen, 1934.

1933 the KPD had formally cut off all association with the group, and Reich was excluded both from the party and from the International Psychoanalytic Association. Sexpol spoke directly to the workers, through meetings and in written material, the two chief themes of which were consistently housing and contraception. These points were constantly returned to as major sources of working-class misery, and were taken as points of departure for the awakening of class consciousness. For example Reich wrote in his pamphlet for working-class youth, *Der sexuelle Kampf der Jugend*:

The sheath should not be carried in a jacket pocket, because the rubber perishes in the warmth. If one does split, and this is only noticed after intercourse, the girl must wash out her vagina at once with a solution of a tablespoon of vinegar in a litre of water. Young proletarians will object, with reason, that in the circumstances in which they have intercourse, this is impossible. All one can say in answer is that here is yet another reason for not simply worrying about the possibilities for sexual intercourse, but getting to know more about the form of social organization which creates such problems for young people.[2]

Such direct forms of political enlightenment have become more difficult today, and often impossible, because the sting has been taken out of subjectively experienced conflict by the development of pseudo-satisfactions, and because the conflict itself has been absorbed by existing conditions. Contraceptives are cheap and young people can use their cars for petting and intercourse. Even though it is still the case in some late-capitalist societies that oral contraception is only available to certain people, this is not really enough to convince anyone of the necessity for class struggle. The chief reason why the lower social classes of contemporary capitalist societies have less access to oral contraceptives is that the social attitudes of the medical profession reinforce already existing prejudices and reactionary ideas. Moreover, medical attitudes are in their turn moulded into a reactionary cast by the feudal and bureaucratic organization of the medical establishment in these societies.

This relationship is in turn mirrored by the fear – neurotic in its degree but well-founded in its origin – which lower-class people have of any medical treatment. This fear can however only be broken down by social medicine campaigns with a democratic, not a public health, orientation. It cannot be overcome simply by basic sexual instruction since this, in present circumstances,

[2] Wilhelm Reich: *Der sexuelle Kampf der Jugend* ('The Sexual Struggle of Young People'), Verlag für Sexualpolitik, Berlin, 1932, p. 22.

invariably terminates in the inculcation of mental attitudes rejecting free sexuality. In the most advanced capitalist countries oral contraceptives are offered freely for sale, e.g. in drugstores in the USA. It would be reactionary to combat this new advance, but it does take away a large part of the directly revolutionary political force of the demand for sexual liberation, that is to say, the demand for an improvement in the technical and social conditions for the practice of sexuality. In this particular case the demand has been absorbed by the system of partial satisfaction. The scope of demands for sexual liberation on this front is now limited, as the following example demonstrates – yet it is the only existing method of direct political agitation. An intelligent middle-class young person has no difficulty in finding a doctor who prescribes contraceptives; in fact the chief media for mass social and sexual conditioning, from which she is liable to derive her social norms, already openly publicize the best means of obtaining them.

Let us concentrate for a moment on this example: the progress from mechanical contraceptives, which are of poor quality and expensive for young working-class people, to the pill. The pill is in principle obtainable for everybody; it is reasonably cheap and absolutely reliable. Yet in some culturally backward countries, significantly, it has remained a social symbol confined to an exclusive minority. When the High-School Students' Action Centre was forming and was engaged in building up local groups, it drew a large amount of its political publicity in schools, and in the community at large, from the demand for free access to the pill for all young people past puberty. This could not help but bring about a negative reaction.

Firstly, the barely established foundations of a joint political platform for high-school students and apprentices (i.e. those at technical schools) were shattered. The high-school students formulated their demands in a way that made it only too clear to the technical-school students that there was a social gap between them, and the division was further aggravated by the young workers' sexual envy of privileged high-school students.

Secondly, though the high-school students are more directly under the control of the social institutions governing them, in so far as their sexual life is concerned, than any other group of their age, they would seem at the same time to form a sub-culture which – due to its intellectual training, its particular emotional bias, and its distance from the pressures of material production – should be most readily capable of insight into its own sexual oppression. In fact, however, they were only influenced for a space of a few weeks by the politically orientated campaigns organized locally in their schools and towns. Of course this indicates that high-school students also are repressed in their sex lives, but it also indicates, even more clearly, that the sexual morality of society and the sexual behaviour of the individual can only become the source of personal political enlightenment – and, after that has been achieved, spur the individual on to a wider-ranging and ultimately class-conscious political commitment – when backed by political enlightenment, reflection and action in other social spheres. The initial 'sex' discussions organized by the AUSS in the individual schools drew a crowd everywhere, but this interest soon fell off. It was certainly true – and this is fundamental – that the initial effect was a strong one. But its power to lead on to wider things, in political terms, had been overestimated.

It was possible for Wilhelm Reich in his day to link every demand for the liberation of sexuality from the complex of forces oppressing it under the capitalist system, with a political demand which struck explicitly at the economic roots of the system. For it was an objective fact that at that time every move towards free sexuality was either openly repressed or hindered by immediately visible causes such as the housing shortage and the expense of contraceptives. The economic, physiological *and* utopian function which Reich gave to sexuality in his conception of how human liberty was to be achieved was doubtless unacceptably mechanistic in many respects, and some of the conclusions he came to were demonstrably wrong. Moreover, it has to be recognized that in today's context it is difficult to relate quantitatively greater sexual freedom to radical and class-conscious demands, and in many cases this has become historically impossible. At the same time it has become very much more difficult to make the qualitative distinction between apparent and real sexual freedom.

Analysis of the class antagonisms in the pre-fascist era could point to three clearly defined social classes: proletariat, petty-bourgeoisie and ruling class. With the advance of monopoly capitalism the large majority of the petty-bourgeoisie were economically absorbed into the proletariat, while ideologically playing the role of functionaries for the ruling class. They shared ruling-class attitudes, or at least attempted to do so, and acted in its interest, either in practical economic terms as the 'straw-bosses' between the ruling class and the oppressed class, or as its ideological agents: retailers, teachers, officials and employees.

The workers' organizations recognized this by concentrating on the 'real' proletariat, especially its hard core of industrial workers, in the build-up of political forces for the class struggle, and by laying the chief stress in their agitation and propaganda on the *antagonistic* contradiction between ruling class and proletariat. In doing so, however, they neglected, theoretically and practically, the 'anachronistic' section of the ruling class, the petty-bourgeoisie. In their theory, the workers' organizations either ignored the petty-bourgeoisie altogether, or else assimilated them unconsciously to the ruling class, simply because they voted, thought and spoke the same way. In their practice, they either paid no attention to them at all or rationalized the problem by relegating them to a 'later stage' of agitation, only requiring attention when the 'proletariat' had already effected the revolution.

The German petty-bourgeoisie formed the central psychological and political reservoir of mass support for fascism. The reason for this lay, at least in part, in the inability of the workers' movement to seize on the anti-capitalist aspects of petty-bourgeoisie life and consciousness and mobilize them in a revolutionary direction. In 1930, Ernst Bloch wrote in *Erbschaft dieser Zeit* ('The Inheritance of Our Time'): 'The vulgar marxists are not keeping sufficient watch on what is happening to primitive and utopian trends. The Nazis are already occupying this territory, and it will be an important one.' He reproached the Communists with 'delivering the petty-bourgeoisie without a struggle into the hands of reaction'. After fascism the old confusion in the workers' movement arose all over again. Who could properly be counted as a member of the petty-bourgeoisie? What elements in it were proletarian? Should it in fact be combated like the ruling class, because, objectively, it represented their interests? – and so on. The German Federal Republic was formed: capitalism began to rise again, and the ruling classes took the solution of this problem into their own hands by declaring, ostensibly on behalf of everybody, that class differences – and certainly those between petty-bourgeoisie and proletariat – had ceased to exist, since the entire nation now belonged to the middle class.

This ideological decree has been reflected in the elaboration of pluralistic social theories and ideologies: in political and sociological theory with the purely formal differentiation of social 'strata', in government ideology by lumping together all the inhabitants of the 'free' part of Germany, in the unions and SPD in the simple division between 'employers' and 'employees' and in the KPD in the notion of an *a priori* anti-monopolistic and peace-loving working population as opposed to the masters in Bonn and the Abs' and Flicks.[3] That theoretical attitudes should have received this particular bias has a certain objective justification: the classes have indeed been transformed, and the differences between them are now of a more disguised, less readily visible nature. Looked at in formal terms, it does not make much difference whether one assumes an expansion of the middle classes, whether, like the majority of critical social-ists, one talks about a 'new working class', meaning every 'manual, intellectual or white-collar worker who is . . . cut off from what he produces',[4] or whether like the new dogmatists of East Germany, one considers that manual and white-collar workers, because of their shared relationships to the proces of production, both belong to the working class, thus leaving this concept as full of contradictions as ever. The debate over the concept of class only becomes meaningful when the purpose is to explain why these variants were coined, what the oppressed class really does suffer from, what it is doing, what it under-stands and does not understand, whether it is fighting, and if so *whom*, to abolish its oppression in order to take possession of its own products, and to understand what it is not supposed to understand.

Only the answers to such questions as these will produce a meaningful conception of class. So, although it is quite correct that 'the existence of the common class enemy produces identity of interest, whether this is generally recognized or not',[5] this truth remains abstract and isolated if the objective identity is not accompanied by an equally objective solidarity among those concerned. And this only comes about through the class struggle.

The workers' movement of the previous generation was able to conceive a variety of practical applications of the formula 'Expropriate the expropriators'. It is not by chance that in the countries of late capitalism, there is no class, and not even any socially relevant group among the wage- and salary-earning population of West Germany, who would voice this demand today. Even in Italy, a country described with monotonous

---

[3] Hermann Abs and Friedrich Flick: German industrial magnates who financed Hitler. Both were found guilty of war crimes but were later re-instated by the Allies in West Germany in their former roles.
[4] André Gorz: 'Work and Consumption', in *Towards Socialism*, Fontana/ NLR paperback, 1965, p. 348.
[5] Kurt Steinhaus: *Zur Theorie des internationalen Klassenkampfes* ('Theory of International Class Struggle'), Frankfurt, 1967, p. 8.

regularity as having preserved the older kind of workers' movement, the people who protest against the war in Vietnam are chiefly intellectuals and young people, who because of their social background cannot be included under the heading of traditional working class. Today in all late capitalist countries, intellectuals, young people and students are to a great extent acting as proxy for a class identity of the subordinate classes as a whole which has yet to be established. They cannot exclaim 'Expropriate the expropriators' except from a reflective distance, as exemplified by the demand 'Expropriate Springer'; or else they formulate it in generalized terms, such as the SDS's resolution: 'Break the Power of the Manipulators!'[6]

A change has taken place in the objects of attack. Where once it was direct social exploitation that came under fire, now it is mental manipulation. This change is indicative of a change in the structure of capitalist rule itself. Not that manipulation has replaced and cancelled out exploitation. But it becomes evident, when one observes the manipulation of needs, and of situations producing pseudo-satisfaction in the commodity market, in communications, and in sexuality, that exploitation is not now confined to its direct physical form but relies upon a gigantic apparatus of created needs which are constantly being manipulated to get people to comply with meaningless social goals. Even the structure of exploitation has changed. The classic structure was: minimization both of primary needs (food, clothing, sexuality) and of secondary needs (free time, sport, etc.), with, *in contrast*, maximization of exploitation (low pay, long working hours, accelerated work tempo, women and children at work, very few social benefits or none at all). The present structure is: manipulative optimization of needs which accord with the needs of the system, abolition of the difference between primary and secondary needs, and *thereby* maximization of exploitation.[7]

In the days before fascism it was the proletariat (chiefly the industrial workers) who seemed destined, through their position

[6] Resolution of the 22nd Delegate Conference of the SDS held in Frankfurt in September 1967, reprinted in *Neue Kritik*, no. 44, p. 34.

[7] See Gorz: op. cit., pp. 347–8: 'As Marx foresaw, advanced capitalism has found itself confronted with the problem of moulding human subjects into the shapes required by the objects it has to sell. . . . It has resolved this problem by conditioning people to what is most profitable to produce – not only in respect of their personal needs, but also in the way they see the world, the way they conceive the state, society, civilization and its co-existence with other societies and civilizations.'

in the process of production, to become subjectively aware of the exploitation basic to capitalism, make it objectively visible through the class struggle, and finally wipe it out through revolution on the whole of society's behalf. But today, because of the increased sophistication of the methods of exploitation and the masking of class divisions, another link has to be added to the chain. This link provides the answer to the question which embarrasses even those who claim elsewhere to hold most firmly to their belief in the working class, and who tend to answer it in evasive rather than in concrete terms.

Steinhaus's answer, to be found in the conclusion of his 'Theory of International Class Struggle', is as follows: 'In all capitalist countries at present a politicization process is visibly affecting intellectuals and young people. This results from their having become aware, whether directly or indirectly, of the barbarism of the colonial counter-revolution.'[8] This assessment is right in itself, but the people who have become politicized belong to no special class. It is of course by no means essential that the fighting class should always have its centre in the industrial proletariat. Such a demand would not only be dogmatic and unrealistic. It would, if one takes the experience of the Chinese, the Cuban, and the Vietnamese revolutions into account, seem to be largely wrong. The young people and intellectuals now in combat with the system are objectively the vanguard of the subordinate classes in that they are acting *on behalf* of all of them. But at the same time they stand in opposition to these classes in that the latter remain integrated by force of the manipulation practised on them. The vanguard are at present in the position of having to fight the false consciousness, that is to say the psychological and intellectual backwardness, of the others.

According to Lenin's theory, the masses and the vanguard are held together by their common class interest, and *relatively* differentiated from each other by the way they perceive that interest. But the change in the structure of exploitation has tended in the present day to turn this relative difference into a potentially absolute one. From feudal times until close on the present day it was always possible to point to the actual source of oppression; it was there, in concrete and immediately experienced form. But with the historical progression from direct exploitation to manipulative exploitation this is no longer possible. Today the concept of 'oppression' no longer denotes specific persons but an impersonal situation: the whole set of

[8] Steinhaus: op. cit., p. 101.

circumstances which permits the barbarity of killing indiscriminately, and on a massive scale, from an aeroplane with no personal contact with the enemy. Similarly impersonal is the oppression by which the ruling class is in a position to dispense satisfactions at will to the rest of society: satisfactions which range from the real, through the pseudo, to the wildly unreal. Those groups (chiefly intellectual) that protest against this contemporary form of exploitation are therefore also constantly in protest against a system of illusory satisfactions and freedoms which the ruling classes allow the ruled to enjoy, without the latter recognizing them as illusory. The subordinate classes react in the first instance to such protests by deliberately dissociating themselves from the political movement, often at the very moment when they are coming to recognize that an economic conflict exists.[9]

This isolation from the body of the subordinate classes is at present a basic aspect of all radical opposition movements. For this reason their results are profoundly ambiguous. It can be argued that this isolation represents a weakness in the vanguard's political programme; certainly it is not simply a case of tactical mistakes. Mistakes there are, in abundance. Examples frequently cited are the incomprehensible language, the provocative life-style, clothes and gestures affected by the protesters. But at the same time all these manifestations are necessary to bind the anti-authoritarian camp together and enable it to find a voice. The incomprehensible language, repellent clothing and irregular life-style are in themselves a protest against manipulation, a first stage through which the group learns to recognize exploitation and to combat the conditions producing it.

At the same time, the movement cannot deny its origins – predominantly petty-bourgeois in the strict sense. It is true that the traditional ideological paraphernalia which used to define the petty-bourgeoisie within the middle class has been falling apart in recent years and only continues to exist in fragmented form. But its fragmented remnants are none the less powerful. For

[9] At the height of the disputes in the rubber industry in Hessen in late autumn 1967, in which widespread strike action was taken, the chemical and metal workers' unions organized a protest meeting on the central square in Frankfurt to put their case. The posters prepared for this occasion by the union officials – recognizable as such through being machine-printed – confined their demands to rates of pay. One of the few posters produced by the rank-and-file workers, had on it the words: 'We're not rowdies, we're working men; give us fair play and we'll work again.' The obvious allusion was to the political unrest in the high-schools at the time and the attempts by Frankfurt students to form a joint front with the workers.

example they influence the *form* taken by protests, which contains elements of the structure of oppression which the protests are intended to destroy. Such an element is in particular the 'anti' type of protest against petty-bourgeois behaviour, way of life, and cultural products which is so abstract that its liberating intention is only recognizable through severe deformations. This type of total, but abstract, negation is particularly a feature of certain manifestations in the field of sexual behaviour. In their intention these are revolutionary, but in reality they only succeed in destroying their object theoretically, and therefore only half destroying it. Such a manifestation for example was the demand for the lifting of the ban on incest, and the introduction of group incest in the earlier *Anschlag* group in Munich, whose organ was *Unverbindliche Richtlinien* ('Non-Obligatory Principles'). Another was the unsuccessful attempt to forcibly abolish the bourgeois concept of 'love and fidelity' in the First Commune.

It is the proletarian sector of the oppressed class who most strongly reject such means of subjectively conquering manipulation and class rule. Though at first sight their objections to the behaviour of the 'left-wing rowdies' may seem to be more or less random – 'dirt', 'disorderliness', long hair, dubious sexual practices – underneath there is still the remnant of something else: a trace, distorted almost beyond recognition, of the old resentment felt by the lower classes for the life-style of the 'young aristocracy'. Peter Brückner has analysed this:

Of course sexual repression does not stop at the university gates, and the position of graduates and lecturers inside the university bears an unmistakeable resemblance to that of industrial workers, in that they have no control over their means of production, all decisions related to which are made by the heads of the institutions. But in spite of all this it is an undeniable fact that students and graduates lead a life resembling that of the young aristocrats of the past. Even when they are in a financially disadvantageous position, they enjoy important privileges.[10]

This further aspect of the isolation of the progressive groups is externally determined and so cannot for the present be removed. Their very mode of protest against all forms of irrational class privilege makes it all too plain to their intended partners that they are benefiting from all the privileges they are supposed to be doing away with. The complaint put forward by the 'hard

[10] Peter Brückner, in Agnoli and Brückner: *Die Transformation der Demokratie*, Berlin, 1967, p. 128.

working population' about the students, that 'they have got time for rowdyism', summarizes all the impotent rage of the subordinate class and what has caused it. The members of this class do not see that they are attacking a group which in fact belongs within their own class, while the class for whom the population really performs all its arduous and above all senseless work goes unscathed.

This isolation will not be overcome through an increase in the number of protest groups (to take, for example, the naïve model of so many young people becoming hippies that the resultant drop in consumption cripples the system), through the demand – in itself still legitimate – for a unification of workers' and students' protests, or through any similar propositions. For the existing separation is in itself one of the results of the contemporary form of exploitation, i.e. manipulation. This is why political strategies aimed at getting students interested in workers' problems are not enough – the politically conscious sector of the students has been aware of them for years. The same can be said of strategies for getting workers interested in the motives of student protest, and persuading them of their justification – which students have also been trying to do in recent years but with dubious success. In both cases, an abstract and moralizing element needs to be brought into the argument; such an element has today become a constitutive part of all forms of agitation and action programmes. Even the theory of the so-called traditionalists cannot do without it, whether they be Communists, Trotskyites, or left-wing socialists in the style of the Socialist Opposition.[11]

The chances that the subordinate classes have of winning their struggle can be schematized as follows. The large-scale use of force by imperialism, with its resultant economic crises, cannot but demolish the system faster than improvements in manipulative conditioning and integration of individuals can build it up. Kurt Steinhaus has attempted an empirical assessment of the 'socio-economic consequences of an increase in the international use of force'[12] for the imperialist state system. So far these consequences, he thinks, in agreement with others, only take the form of a 'latent propensity towards a crisis of the capitalist social system'. Every 'deterioration' has so far been compensated by an 'improvement' in the structure of manipulation. It

[11] A bloc of unaffiliated social democrats, tormed in 1968. Also known as the Socialist Centre.
[12] Steinhaus: op. cit., pp. 101ff.

cannot yet be precisely calculated what will be the ultimate psychological effect within the centres of imperialism of the scarcely imaginable increase in neo-colonial barbarism which has led to the most atrocious wars of extermination. The general politicizing and radicalizing process going on among young people and intellectuals is matched by the even greater effects of imperialist terror. Doubtless the hidden terror inherent in the advertisers' command to buy will give way to more open methods of intimidation. But they will not at first be recognized as such; advertising itself will have paved the way.

Only when economic crises overtake the system of manipulative exploitation will the foundation have been laid for the protest groups, today isolated and acting by proxy on the margin of the subordinate classes, to fulfil the function of the vanguard *within* those classes. At that stage, the esoteric and elitist elements of the contemporary protest movements will lose their rationale. Since the most advanced sector of the anti-capitalist movement will be working within, and jointly with, the whole of the subordinate class, and will be controlled by it, there will be no more question of the vanguard having to fight simultaneously for and against the rest.

The whole sphere of sexuality is today biased in favour of the system. Sex is reduced to a commodity, the human body is de-eroticized, and a false sexuality imposed on life in general and on people's relation to their products; the free expression of instinctual drives is turned into controlled aggression. All these forms of sexual manipulation are typical of contemporary economic exploitation, but they are only *one* aspect of it. A purely sexual counter-strategy, or even a counter-strategy whose main bias is in this direction, is not by itself sufficient to wipe out exploitation. The proper place for action with this emphasis is within the total structure of political opposition and anti-capitalist offensive. It should not be something imposed on the structure from without, but must grow up as a part of it.

# Chapter 2

# The Changing Role
# of Sexual Oppression

It often seems as if, thanks to the volume of ethnographical studies available, we know more about the sexual organization of stationary primitive cultures than we do about our own. Of course there are a multitude of stories, reports, and above all jokes about sexuality which have been handed down from the earliest periods of capitalism, and even beyond. But it is indicative of the status that sexuality has been allotted under capitalism that this aspect of the history of our times has not been accepted as a respectable subject for historical study. As a result the literature on sexuality is veiled by the same lubricity and muddled thinking that shrouds its object in real life. Even the more recent books on the subject, which have pretensions to pass as standard historical works, testify how unaccustomed anyone is to handling material of this nature. It is quite evident that though the authors of these works take their subject seriously,[1] they are at a loss how to approach it, either getting embroiled in a random and eclectic mass of information, or else applying schemas of interpretation which, though at least having the merit of being pre-established, are basically unsuited to the subject in hand.

The founders of historical materialism have not left us much on this subject, except a method, and *The Origin of Private Property, the Family and the State*. Their dogmatic Marxist-Leninist followers have up to now had little more to offer. In addition they have taken great pains to exclude innovators[2] from

[1] This cannot be said of the hundreds of histories of sexual *mores* which are intended as best-sellers on the flourishing semi-clandestine market.
[2] The reasons for which Wilhelm Reich was excluded from the KPD were, approximately: 'You start from consumption, but we start from production, so you are no Marxist.' At any rate, such was the statement made by the German Communist, Wilhelm Pieck, in 1932, in an exchange of views with representatives of Sexpol. See Reich: *Was ist Klassenbewusstsein?* ('What is Class Consciousness?'). The communist educationist Otto Rühle had suffered the same fate some years before.

their ranks, and deny them a place in their account of history.[3]

The direction given to character and state of mind by the form of social organization to which a person is submitted has so far most clearly been indicated by the science of psycho-analysis. Psycho-analysis draws its conclusions from the workings of the human body, the abilities and limitations of its mental apparatus, and the culture confronting the human individual. Its categories are in themselves social categories, but they are intimately related to the context in which they are developed. In Freud this is *bourgeois culture*. In his work, bourgeois culture is not so much identified with the capitalist form of organization under whose sway it developed, as seen as the only existing form.

This does not mean, however, that psycho-analysis is not competent to analyse the mode of social production underlying a culture in its relationship to the psychological and socio-psychological, the individual and collective behaviour of the population. On the contrary, there are a whole series of cultural developments which very probably do have an economic basis and an economic function for the present day – for example, the taboo on incest, and the stress on the necessity of monogamy and male social supremacy – but which maintain such powers of resistance in the face of different, and even conflicting forms of social organization, that they appear as *cultural* phenomena which actually in their turn have a considerable influence in determining the different forms of social organization. Secondly, it is possible to point to cultural developments, for example the capacity for abstraction, logical thought, and calculated action (phylogenetically, quite a late development) which have been absolutely basic to *all* the higher types of human organization and to the ways in which people form economic relationships with one another. Thirdly, there are, among the most recent cultural developments, namely those produced by bourgeois culture, some – such as personal autonomy, responsibility, and love and fidelity – which in a higher form of social organization, for instance, in a socialist culture, would not require to be generally abolished, or be 'superfluous', but would only need to be freed from their narrow bourgeois existence. At present they are

---

[3] For instance, there is not a single word on the Sexpol movement in the eight-volume *Geschichte der deutschen Arbeiterbewegung* ('History of the German Workers' Movement') published by the Institute for Marxism/Leninism, Berlin, though other 'deviators from the party line' were not given such treatment.

fettered by the economic demands of capitalism, and only a privileged minority is allowed to enjoy them, and in specifically truncated forms at that.

The contemporary task of psycho-analysis begins at the very point at which the majority of bourgeois psychoanalysts and Marxist politicians consider it should end:[4] the determination of the tripartite relationship between the form of socio-economic organization, the cultural expression and consolidation of this form of organization, and the way in which the individual reacts to both, either by adapting himself to them, or by changing them. In this book, only one aspect of this tripartite relationship is traced: the individual and social manifestations of the sexual instinct; what contribution sexuality makes in our culture to the formation of the individual; how the individuals concerned react in their turn to the social organization; which impulses and possibilities for satisfaction are broken or abandoned in the process; and how these renunciations and redirections feed back into or react on the social fabric.

Psycho-analysis assumes that the sexual drive is present from earliest childhood and has an important part in the child's first acts of self-expression, its early capacity for reacting to its immediate surroundings, the control of its body, and its preparation of what in later life will be called consciousness or ego-achievement. These presuppositions have been empirically demonstrated, though they have not yet been clinically and psychologically tested in their entirety. The manifestations of the sexual urge in earliest childhood are not governed by the child, or experienced by him as sexual tension or pleasure. They arise independently of the child's own volition, as do his other physical or emotional reactions. The ability to control the sexual drive is acquired in the same way as sphincter control (ability to co-ordinate muscular activity, particularly the ring-muscles). This is a *biological* phenomenon, which only occurs when a certain age is reached (like the control of arm and leg movements), but the cultural superstructure – socialization – demands it, mediates it, and endows it from the beginning with specifically cultural forms. The ability to control the anal sphincter develops *bio-*

---

[1] Robert Steigerwald's criticism of Herbert Marcuse in *Marxistische Blätter*, no. 6, 1967, is typically badly informed: 'It is not our intention here to go into a critique of *Eros and Civilisation*, but we would simply say that those theories of Freud's which are the foundation of Marcuse's argument have been proved by research into prehistory to be founded on false historical premisses. Research confirms the existence in prehistory of the social situations analysed by Marx and Engels, but not of Freud's pseudo-historical myths.'

*logically* at a certain age in childhood, exactly when depending on the individual. Only when this stage has been reached can *cultural* controls, such as order, cleanliness, punctuality and feelings of disgust be meaningfully applied. But *which* of these controls is most emphasized, and which are completely ignored (for example feelings of disgust), also *how* they are applied – with a great deal of force, with little, or even with none at all – depends on the general ideas which the society has about itself, and on its socio-economic presuppositions.

If one bears in mind, when considering this process, that the anal zone is indisputably an erogenous zone, i.e. capable of giving sexual pleasure, and that it is therefore *also* a *sexual* zone, we can derive two conclusions that will be relevant to the problems discussed in this chapter.

Firstly, the direction and control of the sexual drive is not susceptible to manipulation *any* how or *any* way. It has to build upon a biological foundation and develop according to laws which, although not themselves physical, cannot go against the biological trend with impunity. If sexuality is, like hunger, an absolutely basic instinct, it follows that it can never be entirely wiped out. Like hunger, it can be temporarily suspended – after satisfaction – for a certain length of time, but unlike hunger, it can be made to do without direct satisfaction for an indefinite length of time, and it can be 'satisfied' in culturally determined ways which are not outwardly recognizable as the satisfaction of an instinctual drive. The process of deflecting the sexual drive from its natural goal which underlies this procedure can be divided into two separate functions: repression and sublimation (for an explanation of these processes, see pp. 48–9).

Secondly, the above-mentioned biological qualities enable the sexual drive to become the vehicle of social faculties and cultural achievements, and in all known societies it does in fact take on this function. In the process, its nature undergoes a fundamental change.

Psycho-analysis has discovered that the human personality goes through a number of stages in the course of childhood – physical development in which different erogenous zones successively become dominant. Each stage has its own specific functions of pleasure and displeasure. 'Discovered' is the appropriate word, for these stages are not just theoretical constructs which might also be useful in a sociological context – though they are that also – but exist because the child really experiences them. The stages, in the order in which they occur, are the oral, the anal, and the phallic. The latter, in so-called civilized, father-dominated cultures, ends with the Oedipus complex, which leads on, in normal circumstances, to a latency period varying in length and completeness according to the individual, in which manifest sexuality is temporarily put aside, and which in turn leads on to puberty.

The oral stage is characterized by the child establishing a pleasure-relationship with the first person from the outside world with whom it comes into contact, its mother. The specific pleasure in this relationship is oral (i.e. experienced through the mouth), derived from sucking the mother's breast or a surrogate (thumb, dummy). At this stage, the individual is still completely dependent, experiencing its pleasures as a simple, undivided entity. It has as yet not developed an ego separate from the outside world (the mother) or separate from the id. It seems very probable that it conceives the mother's breast as a part of itself (unity of ego and non-ego). This phase is superseded through weaning, which forces the child to separate itself from the mother, that is to say, to recognize her as a separate person belonging to the outside world. This separation, whether it takes place early or late, is always experienced as the renunciation of an instinctual desire, and thus as something painful, non-pleasurable; but through it the child gains an ability which is essential for all subsequent education, and for the acquisition of necessary cultural achievements at a later date – the ability to differentiate between ego and non-ego, that is to say, between self and outside world.

In the following – anal – stage, feelings of pleasure originate mainly in the muscles controlling the excretion process. At this stage, the child is beginning to form libidinal (pleasure-oriented) attachments towards the outside world, so one must assume that its ego is already a fairly highly developed entity. The child does something to please the mother (*excreting regularly*). This phase leads on to the phallic, in which the child's genitals are sufficiently well developed, and its capacity for controlled activity is such that sexual, and in principle even orgasmic, sensations can be induced in them by manual means. The child is by then sufficiently socialized to start having love-relationships with the people nearest to it which bear a close resemblance in many ways to those established by adults, more especially in the adult desire to have a child by the beloved person. This wish is shared by girls as well as boys, and does not take account of sex-differences as it does in the adult world. Much rather, the child probably imaginatively endows the mother with a penis. This desire is regarded as inadmissible in almost all known cultures, and is subjected to taboo through the ban on incest. In all bourgeois and what could be designated as pre-bourgeois cultures (though not in some primitive societies) this taboo is put into effect at the time of the Oedipus situation.

At the height of the phallic phase the parents put a ban on sexual activity for an unlimited time (drive postponement), and on sexual activity within the family for ever (incest ban). In those cultures which we refer to as having an Oedipus complex, this process is attended by threats of punishment: castration in the case of the boy. But even this would not be powerful enough to bring about the desired behaviour if it were not underlined by parental attitudes which the child (this time including the girl) interprets as an indication that the female (mother, sister, playmate) is in fact castrated (punished). According to Freud, the whole complex finds its natural resolution (in individuals who develop into normal adults, capable of dealing adequately with reality) in the child's biological inability to perform the sexual act. In order, however, for the latency period to be properly initiated, not only must the parents cease to be regarded as sexual objects, and sexual desire cease to be directed at the child's own genitals, but several other important developments must be achieved for which the foundation needs to have been laid in the so-called pregenital (oral, anal, and phallic) stages. In the following chapters we shall be returning constantly to these developments and the abilities arising from them as the starting-point of our argument.

The prime requirement is that the Oedipus complex should not simply be repressed. All that need be repressed are desires directed towards the parents; the complex as a whole must be more than repressed, it must, in Freud's words, 'be destroyed, pass away'. Freud did not go into this difference in great detail,[5] but it is of very great importance. Repression would mean that the complex did not work itself out, but was simply officially forgotten, did not dissolve but continued to live on underground, subsequently returning in adult life to govern the individual in a pathological (i.e. illness-producing) way. Its effects can begin in the latency period, with the appearance of neurotic symptoms such as compulsive masturbation or the opposite reaction: scratching, nail-biting, bed-wetting. Destruction of the complex means that the typically infantile constellation of dependence on

[5] Sigmund Freud: *The Dissolution of the Oedipus Complex*, 1924, in The Standard Edition of the Complete Psychological Works, The Hogarth Press, London, 1953–66, vol. XIX, p. 173.

the parents, with all its attendant pleasure and fear, is abandoned, and the child becomes free to make higher, autonomous relationships, involving both consciousness and sensual pleasure.

It is also necessary for the relationship to the parents characteristic of the pregenital stage to be abandoned and to be replaced by identification with one parent; in the normal situation, the parent of the child's own sex. This is a central precondition for the later assumption of the male or female sexual role – and, at present, at any rate – the different social roles allotted to the sexes.

This identification is also a precondition for a child forming a greater or lesser degree of independent judgement, and developing a *super-ego*. For identification does in fact also imply the establishment of parental authority, and moral, cultural and social institutions representing parental authority *within* the individual. It is true that the establishment of an independent judgement capable of controlling the individual's acts requires a sufficiently high degree of *training* of the primary ego-functions to enable a super-ego to be built up at all, but the development of a super-ego worthy of the name confers more than the ability to repress instinctual desires. If this remains the only faculty of which judgement is capable, it is quite often pathological, and the super-ego from which it emanates is at once weak and inflexible. Over and above this faculty, the child should be able to protect itself from potentially harmful instinctual desires, and act *independently* of the punishment and reward system inherent in the infantile method of value-judgements based upon parental authority. This faculty is a specifically cultural acquisition. It should not be qualified as repressive simply because its usual manifestation takes the form of the super-ego merely replacing the parental punishment/reward system, and not building up its own system of value-judgements about reality.

In all known cultures with a relatively complicated economic and social organization, the achievements whereby the Oedipus complex is overcome mark the transition from infantile dependence to the foundation of an autonomous self, the degree of success with which this is achieved depending on the individual case. It is at this stage that the development of genital sexuality at last begins, and it is a vital factor for the establishing of an autonomous self that this should be properly carried through. This means that uncoordinated component instincts escaping control (i.e. the pregenital manifestations of the sexual drive, which are seen as partial by comparison with the genital stage) are all subsumed by genital sexuality. In no case should they coalesce. (To do so after puberty indicates an inadequate repression of the component instincts during or before puberty, and is likely to be accompanied by neurotic symptoms.) Nor must they take independent control (this continuation of the infantile stage leads to perversion). The achievement of proper genital organization is very closely connected with a large number of cultural and social qualities, in particular the cultural qualities of fidelity, love, and independence; their correlatives in the logical and cognitive sphere, reflection and 'free will'; and lastly their socio-economic correlatives: self-discipline, creativity and the recognition of supra-individual social forms. These qualities belong essentially to the post-Oedipal genital character; in this book they will not be systematically examined outside the sexual and social circumstances in which they arise. They are closely bound to particular levels of development in material production and reproduction; they do not arise before these are reached, and these levels of development could not be maintained without them. Two examples from so-called primitive cultures with stationary economies will demonstrate this fact.

Margaret Mead cites three tribes in New Guinea[6] who differ widely from each other in the degree of development of various character traits. In one tribe, aggressive traits are completely unknown. If they do occasionally appear in individuals, they are tolerated in a perfectly unaggressive manner by the other members of the tribe (a manifestation of an extremely high degree of tolerance towards non-conformity in general). Two other tribes are unusually aggressive, both in their individual and their social behaviour; they are, among other things, head-hunters. The three tribes live quite near one another, but in geographically dissimilar regions. All three can be classified as 'stationary economies'. Even the most primitive forms of capitalist-accumulation are unknown to them, though they do have a currency (shells), proving that they have acquired enough of the cultural, cognitive faculty of abstraction (in this case the substitution of shells for goods) to make them capable of dealing with a monetary economy.

All the tribes have highly complicated, though differing, methods of putting the incest ban into effect. But they do not have any process comparable to the Oedipus complex which lays the foundations for the formation, later, of genital sexuality.

[6] Margaret Mead: *Sex and Temperament in Three Primitive Societies*, London, 1935.

There seems very little trace of anything resembling the transition, in our culture, from the anal to the phallic stage. What happens during the anal phase, particularly in bourgeois society, has a direct relationship to what, in adult life, is thought of as an individual's capacity for being *orderly* and *punctual* (in emptying his bowels), and avoiding anything improper or likely to cause feelings of disgust (for example coitus during menstruation). This set of reactions is established as anal pleasure is repressed, and the anal pleasure subsequently reappears as orderliness, etc., in which form it provides a powerful model for organizing among other things initiation and continuation of production. There is no reason to doubt that individuals belonging to the tribes described above also go through a stage in childhood in which sexual sensations are chiefly derived from the anal parts. But it is not marked for them, as it is for us, by being linked to cultural attitudes basic to society. What has become for us an anal phase remains for them an insignificant physical step.

In one way the culture of all these tribes seems to have remained at a pre-anal level, namely, at the oral level and – in two cases – with a cannibalistic bias. They immediately eat what they have; they are incapable of even the most elementary form of storage of property, incapable of any form of primitive accumulation. This could give rise to two – contrary – conclusions: that these cultures are bound to continue (until brought to an end by nature or by colonialism) as stationary economies, and to go on reproducing themselves in the same form, *because* the individual anal phase has never been made into a cultural one, and the functions inherent in such a change, which restrict and impoverish the drive towards sensual pleasure, have never been developed. Or: that they can do without the development of a repressive anal character, because they only have to deal with a stationary economy. Both lines of reasoning are wrong in that they presuppose one single cause. If one followed this mode of thought, the whole development pattern of human gratification would simply consist of changes produced either supernaturally or by pure chance. Another, rather similar conclusion, that these cultures enjoy their characteristic *free-floating* sexuality *because* the restraints on the infantile stages of sexual organization were not comparable in any way to the existing culture, would also be false. It is true that a number of modes of sexual behaviour are prevalent in these cultures which for a long time were strictly taboo in capitalist societies, and were connected, in the societies preceding them, with rituals of secrecy of a greater or lesser degree of strictness, for example pre-marital and extra-marital sexual intercourse. But these modes of behaviour are connected with such complicated exogamy rules, and the members of the tribe conform so completely with these rules, that one cannot talk about sexual *freedom*, and even less of autonomy in the choice of a partner. In general one could say that genital intercourse is practised, and in various ways, and that very probably it regularly produces orgasm, but that, seen from the point of view of the structure of the ego, it is not embedded in a genital (post-Oedipal) context, but primarily follows infantile models.

This first example shows that there is an evident connexion between the level of economic development in a society and the techniques whereby the demands made by such a level of development are imposed on the individual and social character. One point which becomes particularly obvious is that the biologically determined phases of sexual development in early childhood can provide a basis for the development of differing, even contradictory, modes of socialization. This does not contradict the claim made at the beginning of this discussion, that socialization cannot come about in *any* way but has to follow rules: it rather reinforces this claim.

The Dogon, a tribe in West Africa who have only recently been studied, provide another example of the results of socialization occurring without an Oedipus situation in any way resembling our own. The adult members of this tribe appear at first sight to acquire, through socialization, similarly complex cultural faculties to those which have been called 'sublimation' with reference to a person in bourgeois society or in classical antiquity (i.e. the reworking, as opposed to repression, of sexual impulses to produce social activities). But this ability 'to react in a sublimating way' – though in all probability sublimation is not really the process involved – is practised in the total absence of all the conditions prerequisite for sublimation in a 'civilized' person. Indeed the civilized person must use these conditions as the actual base from which he projects libidinous (genital) aspirations onto persons in the outside world. The Dogon has even less of an individual ego than members of other primitive cultures, Why?

The Dogon are not attached to individuals, but rather spread their libidinous impulses over a number of people. The original cause for this attitude lies in the behaviour of the mother. She feeds the child at the breast until it is four years old, the most important aspect of the treatment of children being that their every wish should be gratified.

The child has never experienced what it is like to be granted certain things and denied others. It therefore has no fear of separation, and its experiences in early childhood are free of aggression. The Oedipus conflict is lived through in a significantly different manner from ours. Whereas in our culture we internalize our objects of affection in the outside world on a permanent basis, and become attached to individual people, the young Dogon has various methods of avoiding relationships with individuals. The emergence of exclusive attachments is as much feared in their society as the dangers of uncontrolled instinct are in ours. The Dogon have a tendency to check inclinations towards identification and to react instead with sublimation. The ego which develops in this way is more pliable and manageable. It can adapt itself more easily to the demands of various instincts, but is dependent on the behaviour of the partner. The focus of the Dogon's negative reactions is a dislike for exclusive attachments. The egos of the tribe members function like a group ego.[7]

At first sight this description reads like a communist utopia. But the Dogon are not the subjects of their utopian existence. They have been helplessly bound to it since prehistory, totally dependent on the self-perpetuating conditions of production into which they were born. They are absolutely unable to recognize what their system is, to oppose it, or to change it. It is true that their socialization process is extended over a long period, quite without any restriction being placed on instinct, and they are as a result free from aggression. But they are also incapable of forming relationships to individuals. The latter might seem, on a superficial consideration, to be a desirable goal: i.e. that a person should not form relationships to people singly but as a whole group. But the Dogon are completely incapable of *independently* forming stable relationships. The latter is a necessary precondition for every free and autonomous form of human organization. The Dogon is dependent on the attitude of his partner. That in itself is also not necessarily an undesirable criterion; solidarity and communication always arise on a basis of dependence. But the Dogon is also unable to overcome this dependence with a relationship of mutual obligation, and that is

[7] Report on the 23rd International Psychoanalytic Congress in *Kölner Zeitschrift für Soziologie und Soziologische Praxis*, no. 4, 1963, p. 778. See also Parin and Morgenthaler: *Die Weissen denken zuviel – Psychoanalytische Untersuchungen bei den Dogon in Westafrika* ('White People Think too Much – Psychoanalytic Investigations among the Dogon of West Africa'), Zürich, 1963. This is a highly original piece of work, and almost the only example of how psychoanalytic theory and technique can be used to investigate non-European cultures, without imposing European/American mental attributes on the subjects studied (Oedipus complex, latency period, ego-structure, super-ego, etc.).

another precondition for people organizing themselves independently – indeed it could stand as a description of solidarity in the class struggle today.

An analogous combination of desirable and undesirable (for the present age, that is) results of the socialization process would be encountered again and again if one made a systematic analysis of different kinds of primitive community. It is also encountered in every investigation made into the socialization process whereby a child becomes a bourgeois individual. The capacity to *love* is only one side of a coin, the other side of which is a tendency towards neurotic states of being in love. Fidelity is backed by deadening obedient monogamy which prevents the individual from becoming involved in libidinous relationships to a group. Discipline appears in the guise of anal obedience, and *independence* is conditioned by the egoistic competition specific to our society, so that the necessary *reflectiveness* is made dumb and blind. The question seems to be whether in fact all types of social organization, built as they are upon different and independent character-structures, do not necessarily imply a certain degree of reworking of instinctual drives, which from a viewpoint which considers that such drives should be accepted and welcomed as far as possible, cannot but be undesirable.

## REPRESSIVE ROLE OF SEXUALITY IN EARLY AND IN CLASSIC CAPITALISM

The development of capitalism as the prevailing mode of social production was not simply the replacement of handlooms by mechanical ones, of home industries and small workshops by foundries, blast-furnaces and machine-operated factories, or the fact that men had to move from country to town in pursuit of employment. The present advanced stage of the conquest of nature by technology results from a series of 'impulses' spread over several centuries, but at the same time the means had to be found to keep the process going without periodic impulses from outside, and a social personality had to be developed capable of guiding the process while at the same time remaining completely subordinate to it.

In the seventeenth, eighteenth and nineteenth centuries most European countries, after the forcible process of primitive capitalist accumulation, entered the stage of extended reproduction, that is to say the economic process in which an ever-increasing share of the net social product is not immediately consumed (by any social class), but used for the extension of the

productive forces and fed back into the economy as new investment. For most individuals the concept of postponing consumption today, in order to consume tomorrow, was exactly the
same as putting off consumption altogether. It was all the more
necessary to anchor this process in the national social personality,
in so far as there were no existing social rules to guarantee the
requisite attitude; nor did it make sense to the people at the
bottom of the productive process, who had never had enough to
consume anyway. But it would certainly be wrong to suppose
that only the upper or, alternatively, the lower social classes
were affected by this process, or by the personality changes it
entailed.

The whole complexity of what appears in retrospect as an
economic and technical revolution on the most massive scale,
could only have been possible under the protection of a system
of coercion which did not primarily take the form of chains,
hunger and the workhouse for the producer who did not comply.
Such external forms of coercion would not have been reliable
enough for the process of capital accumulation; they had after
all always been there. The system had to be protected as effec-
tively as possible, all the more so when it began to suffer set-
backs in the form of economic crises, and when these became
more and more frequent. In addition to external force, an inner
compulsion was needed which would be sufficiently powerful to
wipe out all recollection of previous states of relatively greater
satisfaction (namely the identity of production and consumption
in stationary economies).

*The equivalent of childhood + infant amnesia*

Previous historical periods and economies had not, of course,
been without their forms of internal compulsion. But we are
dealing here with an exceptional type. Its objective effect is to
reduce all human activities and qualities to their relative value
for the production process, whereby they also become mutually
interchangeable for things of an equivalent value. The subjective effect is to make the individual feel that nothing in the
world has an independent value except work and the exertion
and suffering connected with it, and, on the other hand, its
corresponding rewards. All other activities are either 'turned
into' work (such as eating, or going for a walk to digest one's
food, or having sexual intercourse), or else are placed in a direct
relationship to work, as manifested in such sentiments as the
following: '*As reward for his work,* and his many years faithful
service to the firm he was at last able to marry the boss's daughter
...'; or, '*Instead of working* he spent his time in bed with a
widow'.

The individual character who has taken this compulsion most to heart, and embodies it most perfectly is described by psycho-analysis as the *anal type*. Freud, in a short description of libidinal types, characterizes this personality, which he also calls 'the obsessional type' thus:

It is distinguished by the predominance of the super-ego, which is separated from the ego under great tension. People of this type are dominated by fear of their conscience instead of fear of losing love. They exhibit, as it were, an internal instead of an external dependence. They develop a high degree of self-reliance; and from the social standpoint they are the true, pre-eminently conservative vehicles of civilisation.[8]

Some years later Erich Fromm also examined this character-type, this time in the shape of the petty-bourgeois with tendencies to fascism, and formulated the concept of the *author-itarian-masochistic character*. Fromm pointed out that people of this type were bereft of the independence, which had previously been the distinctive characteristic of the bourgeoisie, at the time of the economic depression and the increase in the mono-polization process, with the result that they exchanged their conservative leanings for fascist ones.

This concept of the anal character defines at once a certain kind of person, and the dominant social characteristic of capital-ist society. It has its own neuroses, whose symptoms are various kinds of compulsion (for example obsession with numbers, compulsive washing, etc.) which naturally do not arise in all individuals of this character-type in manifest form. The symp-tom disappears when the conflict is absorbed into the character.[9] Analysis of the origins of compulsive neuroses show that the afflicted person generally suffered in childhood from being forced to renounce his instinctual urges at the pregenital stages, particularly at the anal stage, in an abrupt and unloving way; the change did not take place organically. The people who brought the child up (normally, the parents) were in themselves inclined to compulsion, and pushed through the change by force. The child who later develops an anal character had at that time no choice but to completely repress those instinctual desires, with-out having the chance to acquire a pleasure-ego. Without such a pleasure-ego, the child does not have a basis for acting independently and discriminately in repressing instinctual drives, nor will it be capable later of making the decisive choice

[8] Freud: *Libidinal Types*, 1931, op. cit., vol. XXI, p. 218.
[9] See Wilhelm Reich: *Character Analysis*, New York, 1961.

as to whether to repress, wipe out, or simply postpone instinct-ual drives, or learn how to handle different drives in different ways.

It is characteristic of the anal type that the functions of the ego which should develop from the reworking of anal pleasure, i.e. the various tendencies towards order and regularity which are built upon the acquired faculty to control bowel movements, are imposed on a child in a particularly rigid, ruthless and un-yielding way. Clean, conscientious and socially intimidated parents are never so aware of their child as an as yet unsocialized, instinctual being, as when they observe how strong are its anal pleasures, and how obstinately it insists on treasuring the pro-ducts of these parts of the body. When a child is roughly driven away from these pleasures, its ego learns its new functions in distorted form. The later manifestations of this distortion are exaggerated punctuality and conscientiousness, an inhibited attitude in approaching sexual objects, and a great lack of flexibility in all the individual's acts.

*masturbation?*

This is more an ideal type of the anal character than a descrip-tion of it as it appears in reality. In few cases is it so consistent, and more especially the relationship of anal phase and compul-sive symptoms (or character) is not so straightforward as it is described here. Psycho-analysis of people suffering from grave forms of obsessional neurosis has shown that the damage seems to have been done at the transition period from the oral to the anal phase. But exposition of the problem in this way points up the issues more clearly. Sexuality is persistently formed under the sway of the anal character and the economic principle under-lying it. Sexuality appears in real life as something divided from work, and yet which can only be reached through work. It takes on the character of a reward, like good food on holidays, late rising on a Sunday, like money altogether. This reduces sexu-ality to the level of a work process. It becomes, like work, low, dirty and mechanical, and measurable by categories of achieve-ment which have nothing to do with pleasure.

Sexuality is primarily measured quantitatively, as an *exchange-value*,[10] according to how potent the man is: how much he can

[10] That this manifestation of sexuality has an economic cause is confirmed by, among other things, the change that took place in the treatment of sexuality in literature in the transition from the Middle Ages to the Renaissance. It was only with the Renaissance, which was, according to available indications, much more restrictive in sexual practice than the Middle Ages (a change most probably not confined to the ruling class) that a 'quantitative' attitude to sexuality appeared in literature. Masculine potency and feminine desire

'clock up' in a given space of time, how many women he has 'had'. Or for a woman; how many offers of marriage she has refused, how often men turn in the street to look at her, how frequently she is accosted. In being endowed with exchange value, however, sexuality is deprived of all value of its own. It is assessed, secondarily, by its *procreative* function.

The less of an intention to procreate that can be attributed to a sexual act, the more strongly will this act be regarded as 'perversion'. Thus even oral-genital intercourse is often regarded as a perversion although it is not formally (legally) punishable. With a certain amount of goodwill it can after all be interpreted as preparation for normal heterosexual intercourse. Masturbation stands condemned by the procreation criterion, and though in most cases it is not punished in a court of law, schools, boarding schools, prisons, etc., treat it with the utmost severity. Even so, excuses can be made for it on the grounds that it is done out of need, when 'circumstances' allow no opportunity for coitus. Homosexuality, finally, which is completely free of any intention to procreate, is still often treated as a legally punishable perversion. The severity with which it is viewed increases the further the circumstances in which it is practised are removed from a 'marriage-like' situation. 'Stable' homosexual relationships (i.e. those resembling marriage) are less severely punished than 'casual' ones. Anal intercourse is liable to bring about an even heavier sentence in a court of law, when it appears in the evidence in a homosexuality case, than oral-genital intercourse. The reason is ingenious but clear: the guilty parties had the insolence to indulge in a non-procreative act which none the less bears a mocking resemblance to the real thing, thus adding, as it were, insult to injury.

*Love* appears not to belong in the same context as sexual acts. It is separated from sexuality, and endowed with an aura of

---

were measured by the number of times people had intercourse, for how long, and with how many different partners in one night. Morus points out in his *Eine Weltgeschichte der Sexualität* ('A World History of Sexuality', Hamburg, 1966): 'The Renaissance is on the whole a male era. Masculinity no longer has to prove itself by heroic deeds, as in the times of the knights and the Minnesänger, but by sexual capacity, potency. The stress laid on this quality is perhaps the most striking feature of Renaissance erotic literature.' It is certainly not unjustified to claim that this change in function has at least something to do with the transition from a stationary agrarian economy to a colonial and mercantile capitalism. Significantly, this literature originated in the seafaring and capital-accumulating states of Italy and Spain, and not in Germany which was relatively backward.

purity, untouchableness or etherealness. Such a plane is indeed the logical place for it to exist in a social context in which the criteria are performance, competition, and maximization of profits. It is seen as something incomprehensible, outside the ordinary sphere of things, with no real existence in society. This separation places it in contrast to sexuality, thereby increasing the debasement of the latter. The enforced separation of love and sexuality is far from being a matter of ideology, or even interpretation. The classic bourgeois gives it practical realization in his life; in the separation he makes between wife and mistress, ball and brothel, loving care and lasciviousness.[11] The petty-bourgeois imitates him, and the proletarian, while lacking the means to put the former ideology into practice, has no positive alternative to offer. Love remains, in its special, exalted position, as utopian an ideal as the promise of freedom which is constantly dangled above the heads of the whole community. It is exalted into an ideal which must never be united with reality.

*Sexual education* in our time is the true mirror of the contemporary attitude to sexuality. The degradation of sexuality in real life finds its counterpart in the sinister prejudices evinced in official and conventional pronouncements on sexuality. Further proof in terms of examples is unnecessary at this stage;[12] sufficient to say that the official and conventional sexual education of our day is working with means which are not only far behind the contemporary level of technical and social knowledge, but indeed constantly run counter to it. In any other branch of medicine, claims such as those made about the danger of internal infection if sexual intercourse takes place during menstruation, or the destructive effect of masturbation on spinal marrow, would have been rejected by the most backward country doctor a hundred years ago. Other types of claim, such as the numerous pronouncements on the natural inferiority of woman, or of the specifically female character, can at least boast of a greater 'faithfulness to reality', seen in the light of the

[11] In terms of individual development, the bourgeois remains stuck at the commencement of the so-called negative Oedipal stage, and is thrown back upon it in adult life. He never learns to overcome the directly sensual orientation towards the parents, and to transfer it onto other people. His emotional attitude veers sharply between extreme undervaluation of and extreme veneration for the object of his love. Woman is for him either a whore or a saint. See Freud: *On the General Tendency to Debasement in the Sphere of Love* in *Contributions to the Psychology of Love II*, 1912, op. cit., vol. XI.

[12] A compendium of examples, which appear even today in sex-educational literature for the 'backward' classes, is to be found in the first part of Reich's *The Sexual Revolution*, New York, 1969.

whole context of mystification inherent in early and advanced capitalism.

In this age of 'the triumph of science and technology' public opinion remains tinged in many quarters by the sexual practice and ideology of pre-capitalist society, much of which cannot be otherwise qualified than as 'magical'. A telling example is abortion, which is practised at the unofficial level in ways that sometimes bear a close resemblance to witchcraft.[13] The survival of these remnants of archaic culture has been facilitated by the fact that the old interpretation of sexual matters laid down by the Church, as the predominant cultural power of pre-industrial society, has never been consciously brought up to date by the ideology of the contemporary secular state – and with good reason. This typical kind of regression to the ideology of previous historical epochs will come up again when we deal with the way in which the function of sexuality has been manipulatively transformed in the present late-capitalist era, and how new ideological means have had to be found to uphold the necessary sexual taboos.

Attempts at anti-official sexual education and anti-conventional sexual practice often suffer from an unintentional identification with the thing they are fighting. The romantic movement and the youth movement, romantic literature, and a large part of bourgeois realism were always marked by what Wilhelm Reich described as insufficient libido; their sexually progressive impulses had been too much weakened by the ruling reality principle for them to be able to combat the tendency towards repression in their own sexuality, their own sex-denying impulses. Wilhelm Reich described the 'inconsistency of present-day sexual education' thus:

It has the following characteristics: it is always too late, it behaves mysteriously and it always evades the essential point, sexual *pleasure*. Those people who are against any sex education are more consistent. They have to be fought because they are enemies of scientific truth and consistency, but, in a way, they are more clear-cut than those would-be reformers who actually believe that they are changing anything with their teachings.[14]

The situation today is somewhat more complicated. None the

[13] In Paul H. Gebhard and others: *Pregnancy, Birth and Abortion*, New York, 1958, p. 194, there is a list of the 'drugs' most frequently used in abortion: tannic acid, aloes, ergot of rye, saffron and quinine are among the less alarming.
[14] Reich: *The Sexual Revolution*, p. 114.

less Reich's simple, militant statement remains valid. No sexual reformation is possible without social revolution:

The sexual crisis of youth is an integral part of the crisis of the authoritarian social order. Within this framework it remains unsolvable on a mass scale.[15]

The repressive function of sexuality and sex education in early and classic capitalism can be summarized thus: the capitalist mode of production cannot be made to work without a performance principle so firmly anchored in the mental structure of the individual that it does not need to be constantly imposed from without, but works as a compulsion from within. The principle first had a meaning for those groups who initiated the capitalist mode of production, began the process of primitive accumulation, and thereby rose to become a ruling class. For the time being it had no relevance for the lower classes who were still repressed by the brutal, external methods that had always been applied to them. Under the rule of the performance principle, definitive restraints had to be applied to sexuality. Significant sectors of sexual pleasure, especially the pregenital components, had to be tabooed, and the remaining 'legitimate' sectors of sexual pleasure had to be weakened and divided. Only the genital sector of sexual functions and practice was permitted, and this was oriented towards the ideal of monogamous heterosexual intercourse. Meanwhile the repressed components were turned to the service of social integration and the labour-process, and open expressions of sexuality, even if legal, but especially if illegal, were hedged around with a mass of threats, warnings and punishments. All this had the effect of endowing them, too, with a certain 'social utility'. Of course capitalism cannot be *exclusively* blamed for these restraints and repressions, but it was capitalism that first produced them on a world-wide historical scale and brought them to their present degree of perfection.

## MANIPULATIVE INTEGRATION OF SEXUALITY IN LATE CAPITALISM

But just when it is 'brought to a head, it topples over', wrote Friedrich Engels in his analysis of capitalism, *Socialism: Utopian and Scientific*. If a slackening in open sexual repression and an increase in the scope for sexual liberties were a certain sign

[15] Reich: op. cit., p. 115.

that a dramatic reverse was imminent, Marx and Engels would already have said the last word.

The theoretical prognosis of the 'toppling over' of capitalism into socialism was based on the conclusion that the laws immanent in the capitalist mode of production would themselves bring about its collapse. The theory was that capitalist overproduction would increase to such an extent, the amassing of social riches would become so vast and so automatic through the technical improvement of the productive forces and their adjuncts, that a polarization would be set in motion which would cut away the roots of the capitalist production, competition, and exploitation. At the 'end', before the 'toppling over', an ever-increasing population of proletarians would face a small majority of capitalists. While social riches grew, fewer and fewer people would be allowed to enjoy them, all the wealth being distributed by the dwindling number of capitalists or agents of capital (managers), chiefly among themselves. By this time, the capitalist structure would have been so weakened by forces inherent in itself that only a small push would be needed for a revolution to destroy it altogether. But this is where Marx and Engels unquestionably underestimated the capacity of those in power to safeguard the processes of capitalist production and reproduction. With monopoly capitalism, a vast number of methods have been developed for increasing the scope of exploitation and ensuring that power remains in the same hands. These methods are so sophisticated that the writers of the nineteenth century were quite unable to conceive of their effects. Certainly they were correct in their analysis that capitalism was bound to follow certain objective laws, but they could not foresee how imperialism would act in stabilizing the system.

The capitalist economy is protected by such means as counter-cyclical policies, incomes policies, planned restriction of production in certain sectors, artificial creation of jobs, deliberate restrainment of automation in many branches of production, etc., as well as by a gamut of techniques of domination which in the days of competition, or even the early period of monopoly capitalism, were quite unknown. Fascism began to practise the latter methods for the first time on a large scale. One of the uses to which it put the population's instinctual urges was mass destruction. Late capitalism aims to use a large amount of the nation's wealth for increased accumulation of capital (investment), and for products which cannot be consumed (armaments). In forcing the public to comply, it no longer relies on competitive capitalism's chief method of putting a ban on consumption. This reorganization presents two 'rationalization problems' for the superstructure. Individuals must learn to consume; to consume what the system wants and when the system wants. The classic anal obsessional character must be made more flexible. Secondly, the more illogical it becomes to have to produce and consume in this way, the more subtle and imperceptible must the compulsion to do so become, the more 'natural' must the connexion between production and other spheres of life appear to individuals.

The consequences for sexuality can be provisionally summarized as follows. Both real and apparent opportunities for sexual liberty must be increased so that people can say of themselves: 'Look, ten years ago we wouldn't have dreamed that young people would be able to sleep together without fear of pregnancy. Thirty years ago nobody would have thought that youth would be so sexually emancipated, that marriage would have become so much of a partnership, that women would enjoy such freedom, that morality would have become so liberal.' In a word, sexuality is given a little more rein and thus brought into the service of safeguarding the system. The legal attitude to certain manifest (i.e. openly visible) aspects of the public's sexual desires has also been relaxed, thereby allotting them a role in the reproduction of capitalist relations. Meanwhile the latent (repressed) sexual desires of the community continue to play their role as willing or unwilling servants of the adaptation process.

Before going into the various manifestations of *partial sexual liberation* I should like to close this brief summary of the situation by quoting two theoretical accounts of the contemporary relationship between sexuality and class society.

## The End of Rigid Functionalism

In his study of the American student revolts, Lothar Hack puts a question which is of immediate interest to us: what are the causes of the new militancy of the students?[16] Why were the students of the fifties much readier to conform than the students of the sixties, although not so much has changed in the last ten years, and although their 'status uncertainty' and their sense of 'status incongruence'[17] have remained the same? There is an

[16] Lothar Hack: 'Rigider Funktionalismus und neue Unmittelbarkeit', *Neue Kritik*, no. 41, pp. 45ff.
[17] These categories come from Lipset. Their application to the present context is elaborated by R. Reiche in 'Studentenrevolten in Berlin und Berkeley' in *Neue Kritik*, nos. 38 and 39.

answer which can readily be related to the foregoing explanation of why the totally repressive sexual morality of the previous
era has come to an end.

The typical model of behaviour which the middle classes
educated their children to follow consisted in rejecting direct
satisfaction in favour of postponed satisfaction. The faculty of
thinking in long perspectives, and drawing conclusions for the
long term, is developed at the same time as the inability to do a
thing for its own sake – to read a book because one likes it, and
not because otherwise one would not be able to talk about it; to
go out with a person because one likes being with that person,
and not because one wants the prestige of being seen with him
(or her). The classic middle-class education is a preparation for
the 'in order to' attitude – the necessity for seeing every activity
as functional – as 'useful for', 'healthy for', 'a contribution to',
'helpful for'. From the point of view of society this rigid functionalism has indeed been useful, 'functional', in the promotion
of investment and the postponement of consumption. But the
gradual shift from problems of production to problems of consumption that has been going on now for some decades has
radically changed the picture. Sufficient to quote the advertisement for hire-purchase – 'Buy now, pay later' – a motto which
would drive a classic bourgeois to despair. But even from the
point of view of the individual, rigid functionalism, oriented
towards postponed gratification, has become more and more
problematic of recent years since its usefulness as a mode of
behaviour is no longer immediately visible.

It is basically against rigid functionalism that the students are
protesting. The principles of university education have never
been more strongly imbued with it than at present, but it is
becoming more and more meaningless to the students because
it is no longer matched by equivalent restraints in other sectors
of society. The student revolts have a high content of manifestly sexual components, as demonstrated by such slogans and
movements as: 'Fuck for Peace', 'Love-In', 'Kiss-In', 'Make
Love, Not War'. In these protests a 'new directness' is brought
forward to challenge rigid functionalism – but in many cases this
new directness is itself marked by rigid functionalism. Once, for
example, students backed up their demand for the lifting of the
traditional (rigid) ban on boys and girls kissing each other on
the campus and visiting each other in their rooms by a mass
kissing session on the campus. Since however they had for years
been allowed to kiss in cars, in the street, and in the cinema, by
demanding a quantitative increase in 'permission to kiss', all

they probably succeeded in doing was to perfect an already repressive sexual arrangement. It is not immediately visible what is so sexually liberating about kissing in public, especially if the social norms of 'who with whom' and 'how often' are still observed.

## Controlled Desublimation

Freud established in his theory of civilization that the instinctual drives have an essential tendency towards the *pleasure principle*, that is to say, to strive to fulfil themselves in ways as unhampered by the influence of the immediate and general outside world as possible. There are three things however which constantly stand in the way of their gratification: the force of nature, the insufficiencies of the human body, and the imperfection of human (social) institutions. Freud assumed that these three causes, including the last, could never be completely done away with, and that people would always be compelled by them to restrain their instincts. In the course of their cultural development, people encountered these restraints to their instincts in the most varied forms. The pleasure principle could never come to a full flowering; it would always be under the domination of restraints of various degrees, which the individual would transform according to his ability, producing, if he were successful, 'healthy' or, if he were unsuccessful, 'neurotic' results. This whole process of culturally enforced transformation Freud called the recognition of the *reality principle*.

In order to achieve its dominance, the reality principle is forced to submit the sexual and destructive instincts to a permanent transformation. Freud makes a difference here between sublimation and repression. By *sublimation* he means the lasting deflection of an instinct onto social activities which are not directly sexual, but which the individual endows with erotic content. The capacity for 'creative' art is regarded as the prototype of successful sublimation. Sublimation has the important characteristics that it has to take place in early childhood, when the instinct is in its most primal form, and that it leaves behind no pathogenic (illness-causing) traces – it is a 'successful' reworking of the instinct. *Repression* on the other hand is seen rather as the forcible sundering of the instinct from the object of its activity (sexual object), and thus as the thwarting of this activity. The mainsprings of the instinct are covered over – sometimes they remain so for the rest of the person's life – but they continue to survive underground.

In *Eros and Civilization* Herbert Marcuse has submitted the cultural concept of the 'reality principle' to social analysis, and given it two parallel components of a specifically socio-historical nature: the *performance principle* as the prevailing historical form of the reality principle, and *surplus repression*: 'the restrictions necessitated by social domination. This is distinguished from (basic) *repression*: the "modifications" of the instincts necessary for the perpetuation of the human race in civilisation'.[18] Marcuse therefore couples the industrial performance principle with the third of Freud's causes, the 'imperfection of human institutions', and the reality principle in its general form mainly with the second 'cause', the efforts that people have to make against the overwhelming force of nature. People see these efforts as work, and as progress in the conquest of nature (i.e. development of the productive forces and means of satisfaction).

Marcuse himself, in *One Dimensional Man*, makes some

---

[18] Herbert Marcuse: *Eros and Civilisation*, Sphere edn., London, 1968, p. 44. Although Marcuse qualifies the *performance principle* as the historically governing form of the *reality principle*, and thus proceeds to a revision of psychoanalytic theory in the light of historical materialism, this category remains with him basically an *ahistorical* one. In fact what is really necessary is to differentiate between various kinds of *industrial performance principles* and between the various predominant types of social character in primitive cultures, classical antiquity, and West European civilization, i.e. between the historical forms of the reality principle prevailing in these societies. The Roman Empire for example developed a different kind of 'performance principle' from that of classical Greece, and the Mundugumor have a different kind from the Arapesh or the Dogon (see pages 35–6). The *capitalist performance principle* is from a psychoanalytic point of view an *anal performance principle* – a principle which does not inquire 'why achieve?' about any non-sexual or desexualized performance, but only about one which is openly sexual. The existing socialist countries either continue more or less completely in the performance principle of their capitalist forebears or else have not managed yet to overcome it successfully. But the question of differentiation becomes fundamentally important when one comes to investigate the capitalist or socialist accumulation going on in the industrialization of the countries of the Third World. All these countries are in a sense going through the West European 'phylogenesis' condensed into the space of less than a generation, but the way in which they 'catch up' is by building on a quite different socio-psychological basis than their West European models. The various performance principles which develop out of this process will without doubt sooner or later qualify for description as industrial performance principles, but they will be basically different from those of the existing capitalist and socialist countries. The best examples so far are China and Vietnam. Because Marcuse fails to make this differentiation, he is led to oppose the *pleasure principle* to the performance principle in an ahistorical, utopian way, and also to identify this pleasure principle with mythological ideals which could only serve as models of liberation for West European societies, because they could only be effective in the context of the reality principle operative in those societies.

modifications to this simple structure of interpretation which have a central relevance to our remarks about the changed relationship of work, consumption, and sexuality:

It has often been noted that advanced industrial civilization operates with a greater degree of sexual freedom – 'operates' in the sense that the latter becomes a market value and a factor of social mores. Without ceasing to be an instrument of labour, the body is allowed to exhibit its sexual features in the everyday work world and in work relations. ... This socialization is not contradictory but complementary to the de-erotization of the environment. Sex is integrated into work and public relations and is thus made more susceptible to (controlled) satisfaction. ... The range of socially permissible and desirable satisfaction is greatly enlarged, but through this satisfaction, the Pleasure Principle is reduced – deprived of the claims which are irreconcilable with the established society. Pleasure, thus adjusted, generates submission. ... This liberation of sexuality (and of aggressiveness) frees the instinctual drives from much of the unhappiness and discontent that elucidate the repressive power of the established universe of satisfaction. To be sure, there is pervasive unhappiness, and the happy consciousness is shaky enough – a thin surface over fear, frustration and disgust. This unhappiness lends itself easily to political mobilization; without room for conscious development, it may become the instinctual reservoir for a new fascist way of life and death.[19]

At the rally after the International Conference on Vietnam in February 1968 in West Berlin, Rudi Dutschke expressed the opinion that there was no longer any mass basis for fascism in in Germany. Three days later the senate, together with the political parties and unions of West Berlin, arranged a large demonstration to show 'the true face of Berlin'. Eighty thousand people turned up for this demonstration, demanding the crushing of the student opposition and a merciless showdown with the 'rabble-rousers trying to corrupt the nation', and even, as they were gathering for the concluding rally, began small-scale pogroms. It may be true that there is at present no continuous, open fascist movement in the Federal Republic or in West Berlin, but there will be one 'in its own good time'. And that might be any time. At present, and perhaps for a limited period to come, the masses will continue to allow themselves to be ruled by sheer passivity and long-suffering, that very thin – but at present impermeable – surface layer sealing off the fear, frustration, and disgust beneath. But the fear and pent-up aggression could one day become so great that they have to

[19] Herbert Marcuse: *One Dimensional Man*, Sphere edn, London, 1968, pp. 70–2.

'work themselves out' politically; this would be a 'spontaneous' fascist movement from below. Or, the regime could become so unstable, for political and economic reasons, that it has to step in and break the surface (this was the case with the West Berlin senate in February 1968); this would be fascist mobilization from above. The techniques of manipulative rule used today are a necessary condition for the functioning of the capitalist social system without open fascism, but this is not sufficient grounds for claiming that fascism has been historically overcome.

# Chapter 3
# The Enforcement of
# Sexual Conformity

Under late capitalism, the primarily repressive and the primarily manipulative components of sexuality intermingle in a way that is characteristic of the whole epoch. In the first part of the previous chapter I indicated that society is manipulated into sexual conformity by a whole series of methods, some of which date from quite far back in history. I should now like to investigate some of the most important of these 'methods'.

The expression 'a whole series of methods' is an inadequate description for what is happening in so far as it assumes deliberate action, as though there were somewhere a manipulator pulling the strings. What we are in fact discussing is a powerful social tendency. The word we are forced to use, significantly, is feeble and imprecise compared with the potency of the phenomenon it covers.

### DIFFERENCES IN MALE AND FEMALE SEXUAL PRACTICE

It is well known that male and female sexual attitudes and practice differ in today's society. More boys masturbate than girls for example, and more frequently. When girls do masturbate, they very seldom, in contrast to boys, make use of pornography, pictures or other secondary stimuli. Women do not talk so frequently about sex as men; on the other hand they are more ready to give information about their sexual practices (for example masturbation) in answer to inquiries and questionnaires. Men are more given to pre-marital and extra-marital intercourse than women, and are liable to choose a greater variety of partners, etc.[1] These and similar differences have been thoroughly verified statistically; when coupled with psychoanalytical and ethnographic material, they permit a whole num-

[1] See in particular the results of the following empirical studies: A. C. Kinsey and others: *Sexual Behaviour in the Human Female*, Philadelphia and London, 1953; Michael Schofield: *The Sexual Behaviour of Young People*, London, 1965.

ber of relevant sociological conclusions. The most immediate of these is that men, even at their most socially and sexually oppressed, have always occupied the dominant position in our culture, so far as sexuality is concerned. They have inflicted on women, particularly on their wives and daughters, the social and sexual oppression they themselves suffer.

The scope of such conclusions is wide, and there is no doubt that they still apply to the large majority of heterosexual relationships today. It would, however, be a regression to the sexual reform movement of the twenties if we, in the present-day sexual struggle, were to expand our energies attacking such 'inequalities'. On that level, we should be joining forces with women's magazines like *Brigitte* and *Eltern* ('Parents'), for if this is not quite the attitude evinced by the 1968 issues, it certainly will be by 1975.[2] There are signs that even the repressive female image (repressive under the surface, despite its post-fascist egalitarian appearance) created by mass manipulation, especially in the illustrated magazines, is beginning to undergo a long-term change. Six years ago Renate Dörner could still conclude from her survey of 'The Female Image in the Illustrated Magazines' that 'he must be my superior' was the key phrase. She would not find that today in the Springer Press magazine *Eltern*, at least not in so unmodified a form. In the last six years equality of the sexes has advanced considerably, in theory and in real life. The important question is that of the survival, under the surface appearance of *partnership*, of different criteria of performance and pleasure which are considered (provisionally?) still to be indispensable; where, though man and wife are partners and share a mutual trust and love, the man none the less continues to enjoy an inalienable social superiority, which he allows his wife to share more than in the past, but not completely.

The stereotyped ideological attitude now seems to have become: 'In fact we are equal, but I still like to look up to him.' But even this model, which it must be emphasized, is a middle-class one, is liable to further changes in the next few years, though these will not, so far as one can see, lead to an exactly similar type of equality to that now prevalent in America and Sweden. In order for that type of equality to establish itself, a more firmly anchored bourgeois/egalitarian social character would be needed than we in West Germany have inherited from preceding political eras.

[2] An analysis of the content and readership of these and other magazines mentioned will be found in the next section of this chapter (see p. 70).

It is superfluous in this context to discuss the whole range of differences in sexual attitudes and behaviour between men and women which have either continued over from the past, or are in the process of reproducing themselves in changed forms. More, however, than the most 'unprejudiced' observers and sexual reformers assume, these differences are intimately connected with differences inherent in the sexual behaviour of the social classes within which the individuals pursue and reproduce their economic and social life.

## CLASS DIFFERENCES
## IN CONTEMPORARY SEXUAL PRACTICE

The sexual behaviour of individuals is influenced, down to its most subtle and minute characteristics, by their economic position, in particular by their work situation. Once again, various kinds of very broad differences need to be mentioned first: the positive correlation between frequency of masturbation and upper class; early experience of sexual intercourse and lower class; homosexuality and middle class; then the not particularly astonishing fact that the more education and money people have, the more varied are the ways in which they have sexual intercourse, the longer the period of preparatory sex-play, and the more frequently do they make love naked, with the light on, or in the daylight. These differences and their social relevance were first pointed out by Kinsey, whose work remains a classic of popular enlightenment. I only propose here to give three examples of the dependence of sexual behaviour on economic situation.

1. In his inquiry into the sexual behaviour of young people in England, Michael Schofield[3] discovered that not only do young people who are still at school at a certain age (for example sixteen) have less practical sexual experience then their contemporaries who are already out at work, but it also makes a difference what kind of work the wage-earning group is engaged in, at any rate for the girls. Sexual activity is significantly higher among girls doing manual jobs. It has also been noted that sexual activity increases according to the dissatisfaction the girls feel with their jobs. 'Sexual activity', or 'sexual experience' does not however in the least imply that these girls with their more comprehensive sexual experience are happier than their colleagues who enjoy their work more, or their contemporaries who are

[3] Michael Schofield: op. cit., pp. 154ff.

still at school. In fact there is some indication that girls in manual jobs seek sexual contact earlier and more frequently *because* they hate their work, or do not find fulfilment in it, and hope to find fulfilment in the sexual sphere. In this, however, they are unsuccessful, because their work has deprived them of the ability to achieve sexual satisfaction. Schofield's study of the frequency of orgasm did not have a special category for working-class girls. Of *all* the girls he questioned, only 52 per cent answered the question 'Do you like sexual intercourse?' with 'Very much'. The next example will show that most probably the percentage of those answering 'Very much' was considerably lower for working-class girls.

There are no such differences among young men and teenage boys in manual and non-manual jobs. This points back yet again to the problem of the time-lag between women's social and their sexual emancipation immanent in the system. Statistics for *young people in general* show that the rate of sexual experience rises according to the number of times they have already changed jobs (indicating unskilled work), and the amount of their income reserved for their own use (indicating independence from the family).

But in spite of the increased equality between boys and girls in the socio-economic field, the traditional sexual oppression of woman continues. In the case of boys, integration into the working world generally brings about an assimilation of sexuality to industrial standards: increased rate of genital friction (=greater sexual experience) automatically produces an increased incidence of orgasm. In the case of women, it is different. In a sweeping generalization, one could say that women respond to their repressive social emancipation with a collective ban on orgasm.

2. A special study of the sexual behaviour of the lower class by Lee Rainwater[4] provides information on the connexion between social class and a happy sex life in marriage. The Kinsey report had revealed that a woman's capacity for orgasm tends to rise with the amount of education she has had. But even there, doubts arose as to whether a woman's capacity for orgasm depended *originally* on her degree of education. That would be too perfect an example of the 'interdependence of mind and

[4] Lee Rainwater: 'Some Aspects of Lower Class Sexual Behavior', in Ira L. Reiss (ed.), *The Sexual Renaissance in America*, no. 2, vol. XXII of *Journal of Social Issues*, pp. 96–108. The findings in this study are confirmed by J. R. Udry and M. Hall: 'Role Segregation and Social Network in Middle Class, Middle-aged Couples', in *Journal of Marriage and Family*, vol. XXVIII, 1965, pp. 392–5.

body'. Rainwater's main discovery was that wives *and* husbands in the 'lower lower class' had less interest in and derived less enjoyment from marital sexual relations than married people in the 'upper lower class', who in turn had less interest than married people in the middle class:

Table 1[5]

The lower the social status, the less interest and enjoyment husbands and wives find in marital sexual relations

| Husbands | Middle Class | Upper Lower Class | Lower Lower Class |
|---|---|---|---|
| Show great interest and enjoyment | 78% | 75% | 44% |
| Mild interest and enjoyment | 22% | 25% | 46% |
| **Wives** | | | |
| Great interest and enjoyment | 50% | 53% | 20% |
| Mild interest and enjoyment | 36% | 16% | 26% |
| Slightly negative towards sex | 11% | 27% | 34% |
| Reject sexual relations | 3% | 4% | 20% |

Rainwater inquired into the cause of these differences and found it in 'the quality of conjugal role relationships in the different classes. In this same study we found that middle class couples were much more likely to emphasize patterns of jointly organized activities around the home and joint activities outside the home, while working and lower class couples were much more likely to have patterns of role relationships in which there was greater emphasis on separate functioning and separate interests by husbands and wives.' Rainwater classified his material according to degree of role segregation in marriage ('intermediate' or 'high') and came to the simple, but important conclusion that the higher the degree of role segregation in general, the higher the degree of 'segregation' in sexual relations (see Table 2).

These statistics only refer to white married couples. In Negro couples the same trend is there, but the rate of sexual satisfaction is generally higher.

We would enlarge on this by saying that the lower the social class, the more are husband *and* wife burdened by (a) the

<hr>

[5] Rainwater: op. cit., p. 98.

material pressure of the economic struggle for survival which they both experience, but independently of each other, (b) the fact that they have enjoyed too little formal education to be able to develop common interests outside these spheres of independent experience (the upbringing of their children, sport, culture, etc.) – in fact it is much rather the case that they are forced to carry on the divisions of their working lives into their leisure time and their family lives, (c) their own upbringing, which will have taught them very early on – at any rate much earlier than children from the upper class – that the private sphere was something quite different and opposed to everything else, which can only be preserved with a struggle. Rainwater thinks it likely that these economic factors also play a role in pre-marital sexual relations.

Table 2[6]

Lower class couples in highly segregated conjugal role relationships find less enjoyment in sexual relations

| Husbands | Intermediate Segregation | Highly Segregated |
| --- | --- | --- |
| Great interest and enjoyment | 72% | 55% |
| Mild interest and enjoyment | 28% | 45% |
| **Wives** | | |
| Great interest and enjoyment | 64% | 18% |
| Mild interest and enjoyment | 4% | 14% |
| Slightly negative towards sex | 32% | 36% |
| Reject sexual relations | — | 32% |

3. In the middle and upper classes not only is the preparatory love-play before the sex act more varied than in the lower class; it has a qualitatively and quantitatively greater meaning. It must also be remembered that the higher up the social scale, the higher the incidence of masturbation as a source of pleasure, and the more liberally is it resorted to. On the other hand boys and girls from the lower social classes embark on heterosexual intercourse much earlier. Of course lower-class men, and in particular lower-class women, also marry earlier than people of a higher class. But this does not explain the differences. The questions that we have to ask are why they marry so young, and why their love lives lack choice and variety to such a degree. Certainly it

*and, because earlier remains rather stereo- typical. Thereafter.*

[6] Rainwater: op. cit., p. 100.

still remains more important to upper-class people than to those below that one should marry a person of one's own social position, that a girl should be a virgin when she marries, that a girl does not become attached to a young man from a lower class than herself, that an upper-class boy uses lower-class girls for passing affairs only, etc. The upper class have their traditional reasons for this, in that it is a way of maintaining their social and ideological power.

This is, however, far from explaining all the above. Young people growing up in the upper classes have to undergo a longer period of education in school, and they are therefore, according to prevailing conceptions of morality, obliged to abstain in order to be able to learn at all (and not have to leave school or university before they have completed the course, etc.). But even that does not explain why young lower-class people are fairly ready to do without *masturbation*. For we know that boys at any rate become acquainted with it at just as early or earlier an age as their upper-class contemporaries. However, their family circle, their meagre formal education, and finally and above all, their work situation, do not allow them to develop the capacity for reflective and associative thought. But if masturbation is to be an independent source of pleasure, it calls for a faculty which is closely related to that of associative thought – imagination – in a fairly high degree; a faculty, that is, susceptible to conscious manipulation by the person concerned when it becomes necessary. This faculty seems to be a general precondition for all the more complicated forms of sexual satisfaction. This is an important reason why young people from the lower class use masturbation as an 'emergency brake' but not as an autonomous source of pleasure. A great deal of the 'crudeness' and 'lack of eroticism' in the way working-class people practise sexual intercourse can be traced back to a deficiency of imagination, crippled at source by their circumstances.

This is yet another manifestation of the power of the principle of 'abstention from enjoyment, in the interest of later, greater, enjoyment'. This principle affects the lower classes as a brute economic fact. They cannot do anything but abstain. 'Postponed enjoyment', temporary abstention, do not exist for them; they are identical with perpetual abstention. For the upper class and a section of the middle class, the abstention principle – while still remaining rather a cheerless one – does, none the less, produce certain rewards, especially in terms of culture. If things turn out right, the young upper-class person begins to recognize this when he grows up, at the latest when he comes into his inheritance, and he sees that the self-denial which he underwent in his long school education and his early abstention from sexual experience have in fact 'paid off'. But young working-class people do not in general have the chance of a long school education, with its attendant compensations of free afternoons, parties, etc., and even when this possibility is open to them, they cannot understand how the economic sacrifice involved could eventually *benefit* them. It is therefore quite plain that they will not apply the principle of 'postponement of immediate desires in the interests of later, greater enjoyment' to their sex lives, when they have learnt it so inadequately from family, school, and environment. They are much more likely to learn that 'what can't be cured must be endured', and to put everything in society down to 'human nature'. They lose all ability to recognize that they are in a *socially* oppressed condition, transforming their consciousness of their position as the underdog into a generalized cynicism.

Marcuse has analysed sociologically how a repressive desublimation of the instincts has been taking place in recent years. The study of sexual ideology and manipulation in advertising, consumption and the mass media, and the results of empirical investigations into sexual behaviour (though admittedly these only touch on the surface manifestations of such behaviour) lead one to believe that this trend is far less developed in the lower class than it is for the middle class. But it is difficult to draw a rigid dividing line between lower class and middle class, because sexual behaviour does not alter so rapidly as place of work and income. It is (so far) unnecessary to apply methods of repressive desublimation to the lower class to force them to conform with 'the advanced industrial civilization', whereas with the middle class it is necessary. For example, the same degree of restructuring of behaviour is not needed to induce the lower class to consume more, or more of the right things. The command to abstain inherent in rigid functionalism did not traditionally have to be so strongly anchored in the ideological structure for the lower class as for the others, since it was already unmitigatedly present in the economic pressures of their work and leisure. At the same time, however, we should observe that lower-class sexual norms are much more rigid and less open to individual interpretation than are those of the classes further up the social scale.

The fixed, unyielding nature of external norms in the lower class cannot be compared to the traditional rigid functionalism of the middle class. The latter tends to have the function of mediating the process of social adaptation (as does its successor, repressive desublimation), where the former has more the function of enforcing external stability. For the overwhelming majority of lower-class people the work process is so inflexible, depends so little on even the appearance of an autonomous decision on the part of the individual, and weighs so heavily on his thought and behaviour that it brings about an almost complete lack of inner stability (or identity) which has to be replaced by extremely unyielding external controls if the lower class is not to degenerate into a state of complete indifference to all the ruling norms. This is of course a very sweeping generalization, but it is certainly confirmed by study of the 'class' underneath the 'regular' lower class, what the Americans call the 'lower lower class'. The system of rigid moral controls and juridical sanctions does not extend into the subculture of the slums, among the people who have 'dropped out' of the productive process. These groups show a situation so far unencountered by sociology: 'total loss of norms', i.e. an extremely high incidence of schizophrenia, incest, in general of sexual behaviour lacking to an advanced degree in object-identification or personal stability, whether the relationships concerned are heterosexual or homosexual.[7]

## THE CLASS FUNCTION OF SEX EDUCATION

Sex education as it is practised today is a particularly efficient instrument for manipulating people into conformity, and as it is periodically rewritten to suit the 'latest state of affairs' it is a very sensitive index of the progress of such manipulation and the instruments it employs.

In this section we do not propose to investigate the official sex education literature issued by government sources. Nor do we intend to examine works of science on the subject, whether critical or affirmative in attitude. We propose to concentrate on the less conscious and consequently more influential level of sexually oriented literature, from works of the romantic 'Is my Love any Different?' variety to the blatant 'Sex in the Office' type, and on the direct and indirect sexual content of mass-circulation magazines and newspapers.

Conservative cultural critics regard these products as a 'flood'

[7] This has repeatedly been the finding of clinical empirical studies of the relation between social class and psychosis. So far the only in-depth studies of this field have been American.

brought forth by the public's insatiable, unhealthy appetite for them, developed by a profit-hungry minority of commercial interests. The only remedy, as these critics see it, is to erect a wall of education and suitable norms between the public and the source of corruption. Socialist and other progressive cultural critics take the view (basically correct, but often oversimplified) that these products represent a universal trend towards 'false sexualization' (the term was invented by Rudi Dutschke), towards 'permanent stimulation of desire for sex-substitutes'[8] or 'repressive desublimation', universal, that is, except for those members of society who are able to make a conscious critique of society. Where this position becomes oversimplified is in failing to recognize that these processes are implemented by different and sometimes contradictory methods, according to the social class being worked upon. The choice of methods depends not only upon the receptiveness and general level of intelligence of the class concerned, but also on the specific objective of the campaign, i.e. what it is being conditioned *for*. (Without this condition, we should be able to note that the magazines *Twen* and *Bravo* both practise false sexualization or controlled desublimation, but would be quite baffled by the phenomenon that *Twen* contains open incitements to things which *Bravo* warns its readership at all costs to avoid.) But even individuals capable of making a conscious critique of the situation are not automatically safe from these pressures; a special network of agencies of controlled desublimation, with variants for all cases, has been provided for them, and they also manufacture them for themselves.

The seemingly random and undirected 'flood' of sex literature, sexual stimulation through films, fashion and advertising, the articles on sexual matters and events in magazines, and the marriage advice and personal problems pages can in fact be classified according to type of social, sexual and manipulative content and pressure to conform.

1. *The media of social conformity and the instruments of manipulation use a spectrum of symbols and stimuli which work on the pregenital organization of the individual and permanently influence the open and private spheres of genital sexuality.*

Such stimuli are, (a) the *fulfilment of impossible daydreams*: great love in an exotic setting; winning the football pools; making a wealthy marriage and being able to stop work; the

---

[8] A. and M. Mitscherlich: *Die Unfähigkeit zu Trauern* ('The Incapacity to Mourn'), Munich, 1967, p. 290.

possibility of *staying young* and attractive for ever (through hormones, massaging the bust, going on nature-cures); (b) *narcissistic professions* (mannequin, photographers' model, starlet, champion sportsman); (c) *disgust syndrome* and *cleanliness syndrome*: 'since I started washing with x they all find me attractive'; (d) venting of *aggression* on sexually 'free' groups: homosexuals, libertarians, students; (e) mobilization of latent neurotic and manifestly anti-sexual *fear*: cancer in the sexual organs; side effects from the pill. Critical literature of recent years has gone into the effects of these and similar stimuli in a comprehensive and enlightening manner. But they were represented as having the same kind of conventionalizing effect on all subjects who were not sufficiently conscious of being worked on to resist it. This is not the case: these stimuli are aimed at different classes, sometimes at very definite and precisely calculated groups.

2. *The lower the social stratum, the more brutally and openly are the methods of forcing individuals to adapt to sexual and social norms applied; but above all, the norms themselves become progressively more stringent. The higher one is in the social scale, the greater is the leeway for individual deviation and the amount of apparent freedom planned into one's existence by the manipulators and permitted by the ruling class.*

It seems as though a large number of even the most progressive cultural critics have derived their concepts of false sexualization and repressive desublimation from studying the highest social stratum still manipulated on a massive scale: young managers and young male employees in commercial firms, and the upper grade of female secretary; 'middle-middle-class', or even 'upper-middle-class' manipulation. *Twen* and *Elle* ought certainly to be analysed, but in the process we ought not to forget about *Bravo* and *Das Neue Blatt*.

Let us take as an example the currently most influential organ of social and sexual adaptation on sale in West Germany: *Eltern*.[9] This magazine is aimed at young married couples in the broad middle area of society who are just embarking on a stable domestic and material existence. The advertisements, which take up a large proportion of the magazine, are predominantly for household and functional clothing (as opposed to fashions), for easily prepared foods, medicines to build up general health, toys, underwear, and small household articles. There are no advertisements for alcoholic drinks or cigarettes. The magazine is read particularly by wives; articles of 'special importance for fathers'

[9] All quotations are from the December 1967 issue.

are marked with a star on the contents page. Its one leading principle is 'happy marriage at all costs' and great concessions are made to this in the pages of sex information. For instance, *Eltern* appears to be quoting Kinsey in much the same spirit as we have done: 'His inquiries revealed that there are significant differences between the attitudes to sex and the sexual behaviour of different social classes. The difference is particularly clear in the case of nakedness during intercourse and sex play before the act. ... There is even a difference between middle class and upper class. The higher people's degree of education and social position, the more often they prefer to make love naked. ...' There follows practical advice on increasing the pleasure of sexual intercourse during pregnancy: '... or else the man approaches the woman from behind. When pregnancy is far advanced, the so-called "riding" position, where the woman sits astride the man, ought to be completely avoided, since the man's penis can go too far in and cause internal irritation.'

The immediate impression conveyed by *Eltern*'s sex information is very favourable, all the more so since so much of what it has to say is practical and informative. People are indeed being induced to conform (in this case, to the social ideal of marriage), but it does seem like the kind of conformity which our industrial civilization, which has preserved so many cultural remnants from pre-rational eras, can really do with. This is also the opinion held by the authors of the article quoted above, 'Van de Velde 1967', of their own attempt to provide sexual 'further education': 'The aim of this entire report is to get rid of fear and uncertainty by giving clear information.' An explanation of the physical facts of sexuality such as the one quoted above would not have been possible in women's magazines ten or even five years ago. The pressure to conform to a restricted, socially inferior role was still too strong, even for young middle-class women with jobs. In this case, then, there has been, to use Marcuse's definition, an increase in 'the range of socially permissible and desirable satisfaction'. Woman remains a sexual 'object' in a situation fraught with constraints of its own – monogamous marriage – but she has gained a certain autonomy. Even Marcuse would not complain that 'through this satisfaction the Pleasure Principle is reduced'. It might be possible to complain that the pleasure principle was being reduced in this case, in that its application was confined to married women, but in fact other magazines such as *Twen* make it clear that middle-class unmarried girls are also entitled to their – admittedly not quite so substantial – share of the cake.

The reason why this is none the less a repressive situation lies in the very restricted contexts in which the various groups (subdivided socio-economically) are to be allowed their new semi-freedom – 'this and that may only be done in this and that situation'. This does not affect married and unmarried women only, but single men, married men, men in love, working-class young people, middle-class young people, in fact groups of all kinds. Every edition of *Eltern*, and other corresponding magazines, rounds off and simultaneously hedges in its advocacy of the 'new freedom' with similar restrictions. Thus *Eltern* prints a story, intended to complement its other material, about a young unmarried shorthand typist called Renate who was expecting a baby. Her boy friend, the father of the child, was 'French, Corsican to be precise. His mother was Vietnamese. He was an engineer.' Her first thought was to have an abortion. 'I had found a doctor who was willing to do it for me. Then by chance I read *Eltern*. I had my baby. And now I am happy.' In picturesque Corsica of course, delighted with her exotic married name of Grimaldi, and even more delighted with her charming baby, Frédéric. And as if all this were not enough, she now has insight into how it happened: 'Just as I had been touched by wonder, that time in the bathroom, now I had been touched by fate. I realized in this moment that I could not run away from my own destiny any more. I must accept motherhood.'

So much for sex education. So much for the relative danger or harmlessness of medical abortion, the social and legal discrimination against unmarried mothers and illegitimate children, the individual's right to enjoy sex for no other reason than that it is what he or she wishes. Everything is swept away in a flood of wonder, magic, and exoticism. This stereotype occurs again and again in papers like *Eltern*, if not always in quite such explicit form, and from it we can derive a formula for a specific type of manipulation, carried out with a particular social group in mind: any extension of the possibilities for satisfaction is simultaneously counterbalanced by an equivalent restriction on the circumstances in which it can be enjoyed, which is presented as an absolute command ('that I could not run away from my own destiny any more'). The so-called extension is presented as a gift of the manipulators ('Then by chance I read *Eltern*'). This fits in with Marcuse's formulation: 'The range of socially permissible and desirable satisfaction is greatly enlarged, but through this satisfaction, the Pleasure Principle is reduced – deprived of the claims which are irreconcilable with the established society. Pleasure, thus adjusted, generates submission.'

The full extent of this subjection becomes clear when we compare the above example with the 'extension of sexual satisfaction' accorded to other social sectors and age groups. *Twen* centres upon a world of carefree pre-marital sex, fashion, cars, jobs, fashionable French dishes, a sprinkling of culture, jazz and pop, and the numerous other things to which a *Twen*-person can consider himself or herself entitled. No better description has been found of this section of the magazine-reading public than *Pioneer Consumers* which was produced by a readership survey commissioned by the Springer Press itself. From this it can be seen that the *Twen* reader is intended to express his or her youthful rebellion by extravagant acts of consumption. He or she pioneers a whole new world of social conformity which the readers of *Bravo*, *Eltern* and *Das Neue Blatt* have not yet cared to explore, from miniskirts to homosexuality.

The November 1967 issue of *Twen* began its monthly sex-report as follows: '*Twen* wanted to know how difficult it is for unmarried people to get oral contraceptives in Germany. . . . Our results were encouraging. Prescriptions for the pill are no longer at a premium.' Practical descriptions were then given of the best way for a young girl to get the pill. Potential pill-swallowers were even advised on where to go if they could not find a doctor who would prescribe oral contraceptives. 'People who do not have an open-minded family doctor can apply to the advisory centres listed below, where they can get the address of a progressive doctor. Anyone who would also like to have further information about contraception is recommended to send for Hubert Bacia's comprehensive list of relevant literature, obtainable from the SDS, Berlin, Kurfürstendamm 140, at a charge of 2DM.'

So far so good. The politically minded reader will perhaps be surprised that *Twen* (published, like *Eltern* and *Bravo*, by the Springer Press) should be giving publicity to an organization that has been demanding the forcible democratization of the Springer Group. He will perhaps interpret it as a sign of Springer's inner democracy and liberality. Our immediate concern is what the young girl does with the pill when she has got it. In a 'fictional' report in the same issue, an anonymous virgin is there to give the answer. Like Renate's in *Eltern* it has a commanding ring: 'I'm 19, and still a virgin; in other words, I don't want to stay one any longer.' The virgin comes from Bamberg, her fiancé shares the moral outlook of most people in Bamberg in that he would like her to preserve her virginity until their marriage. What does she do? She goes to Munich with the

intention of losing it. What does she discover? That no real man
wants a virgin. 'An innocent who comes to Schwabing to be deflowered is going to be disappointed. The only people who were
interested in me were nut cases, good friends, timid teenagers and
queers. ... I went to bed with Tim. I was terrified, but I
needn't have been, because the minute he discovered I was a
virgin he threw me out. ... I offered my all to a student from
Berlin who rang at the door selling magazine subscriptions. I
went to the door in nothing but a short white dressing-gown.'
Even this did not work. She finally got herself deflowered by a
dumb painter who did it with as much interest in who she was
as 'he had about the posters he was painting all the time, some
for the extreme right, some for the extreme left, any old thing,
depending on what was going'. She ends with the words: 'I've
settled down very happily with my fiancé in Bamberg.'

This typical *Twen* story is only one degree less primitive in its
construction than other kinds of reader-manipulation in *Eltern*
and *Bravo*. But these small degrees of difference are precisely the
significant factor. The *Twen* story is written in a style composed
of exaggerated irony (which distances the readers and makes
them feel superior) and command (which forces them to adopt
the norms of pre-marital sex.) The attitude which this 'ironic
command' imposes on the readers is: sex before marriage, yes;
a fling or two on the side, yes; intercourse without worries, yes –
*but* sex before marriage is really sexuality *followed by marriage*.
There can be no doubt that someone conditioned by this process
will never be able to achieve a complete love-relationship, even
in a later monogamous union. *Twen* readers are kept in a state
which the Mitscherlichs have described as 'a complete levelling
out of the differences between individuals ... (by means of)
permanent sexual stimulation, which is turned to as a compensa-
tion for the ever increasing dissatisfaction that they feel with
having to accomplish "meaningless" work.' It is a real process of
destruction, so far as the individual's capacity for love is concerned. Of course *Twen* and analogous agencies of manipulation
such as films, fashion and the press are not the original instiga-
tors of the trend, they simply consolidate and advance it. *Eltern*
has something of a resigned tone, though it claims to be 'for
life's happiest years', and it and similar papers aimed at the older
age group maintain the destruction process at the maximum
bearable.

In *Bravo*, the only really typical magazine for lower-class
young people, manipulation is not only cruder and more immediately recognizable as such, but the norms to which the readers

are urged to conform are more stringent, so stringent, in fact, that little 'false sexualization' is involved. *Bravo* tends, rather, to hand out rules to its readers about the quantity and quality of sexuality allowed. And it must be remembered that *Bravo* is not only aimed at a different social class from *Twen*, but its readership is several years younger. *Bravo*'s readers are predominantly lower-class people from fourteen to eighteen, *Twen*'s readers predominantly middle-class from eighteen to twenty-six.

*Bravo*'s cultural and moral attitude is one of manipulative conservatism. Chivalry, enjoyment of life and 'realizing when it's serious' are the values it constantly preaches. Some of *Bravo*'s sexual standards appear to run completely counter to *Twen*'s: earn as much money as you can as soon as you can; get married as soon as you can; behave honourably to each other; try not to have too many difficulties with each other; sexuality is not as important as all that; don't sleep together before you're married, but if you do, get married as soon as possible.

*Bravo* has very recently begun to have a weekly sex-report. But sexual standards are either laid down in a paternalistic tone of advice, or handed out direct, as in the traditional women's papers, as answers to personal problems by an 'expert', in this case 'Dr Vollmer'. For example, under the heading 'Sylvia' we read in a November 1967 issue:

*Question*: I'm 17, people tell me I'm very pretty, and I have a very nice boy-friend who is in the army at the moment. My parents don't like us being friends and behave very strangely to him. They don't like him because he is not good-looking and only as tall as I am. In a few words, he's not the type they were dreaming of for their daughter.
*Answer*: If your parents have no other objection to the young man, you should be able to persuade them to take to him. Tell them how at home he always feels with them – even if it isn't true. Tell your father how much he admires him, and your mother how much he liked her apple pie or her new dress. If you pave the way like this, you are bound to succeed in convincing them about him in the end. They they will see that there is nothing less important for successful friendships and happiness in love and marriage than good looks, especially for a man.

The most interesting point about this example is not that the *Twen* reader would find Dr Vollmer's answer ridiculous. *Twen* readers in any case do not have that problem: an ugly partner, or at any rate one not conforming to the current standards of beauty, would be quite unacceptable to them, unless the person concerned had an alluring brand of ugliness which would not be out of place in an advertisement, or indeed the prestigious brand of ugliness actually sought after for advertisements. The really interesting point is the vicious introjection of parental values and the conduct demanded by them. Superficially, the young person seems to be outwitting the parents. But in reality it is not the parents, but the young people themselves who refuse a potential partner on the grounds of inadequate looks. Sylvia projects her own dislike of ugliness onto her parents, and this vicious identification draws her into her parents' field of values. It is as though the young person felt obliged to persuade her parents that one does sometimes have to make do with a less good-looking partner, whereas the really important fact is that she herself has had to learn to come to terms with the disappointing nature of reality, made all the more disappointing by the impossible ideal of beauty and attraction which the agencies of manipulation have wafted before people's eyes, making every normal love relationship seem dull.

Young people from the lower classes get to know the constraints of 'real life' much earlier than middle-class people. For this reason they only make very brief contact with the sphere of sexuality and pleasure – and a very manipulated and largely illusory sexuality at that – before it takes second place to the problems of 'appearances', and of adapting themselves to the world of work and the family. This accounts for the fact that manipulation of this group of young people still works very largely by *combatting* sexuality, and not, as in *Twen*, by *using* it.

A corresponding difference is to be found between the usual types of sex questionnaires and 'love tests' published in these two magazines. The issues quoted above both contain questionnaires, similar in form to each other, the one in *Twen* entitled 'Rendezvous 68', the other '*Bravo*'s Love Test'. 'Rendezvous 68' has many more directly sexual questions than its counterpart (about 15 out of 73, as opposed to 5 out of 100 in *Bravo*), and in addition, it actually provides the opportunity for finding a boy- or girl-friend. If one sends in the results obtained, one gets the address of a 'suitable' person. The magazine warns: 'This is not a passport to happiness. Whether you will be happy together or not cannot be decided by anyone but yourselves.' You are then intended to arrange a date and get to know each other.[10] *Bravo*

[10] One example of class differentiation in such attempts to manipulate the public's choice of partners is the fact that it is considered completely socially acceptable for young lower-class people to choose their boy-friends, girl-

only sends back a computer report on one's personality. 'The computer will give you a careful and honest answer. It will be an entirely personal one, based on the information you have given.'

*Twen* allows a large apparent freedom of choice. For example: 'You are at a party with someone you really like. Suddenly you notice that your partner is flirting with other people. How do you react? 1. I make a scene. 2. I am upset. 3. I begin to flirt too. 4. I'm glad. 5. It doesn't affect me one way or the other.' Of course such a wide range of alternatives is not open to a *Twen* reader in reality, but at least they are put forward as theoretical possibilities. In *Bravo* they are simply not there. The largest number of questions in the *Bravo* test relate to social adaptation. For example: 'A person who has not got anywhere in life ... 1. Is a ne'er do well. 2. Is often very nice in himself. 3. Has just been unlucky.' Every answer contains some degree of condemnation for the 'person who has not got anywhere in life'; all that is measured by the test is the relative degree of tolerance the reader is prepared to accord him.

Numerous other examples could be quoted of the ways in which films, advertisements and different magazines are geared to produce different kinds of social and sexual conformity in different groups; in this context it is unnecessary to go into all of them. The similarities and differences in *Twen* and *Bravo* lead to a second point. Different though their prescribed routes may be, *Bravo*- and *Twen*-people are heading in the same direction: towards marriage, in the repressive, monogamous form demanded by the economics of the technocratic society which for the present at any rate remains the absolute norm for all classes. The lower classes, as befits their monetary status, have to conform earlier, more ostensibly and more unconditionally than the *Twen* reader, and in a way which excludes all possibility of a radical alternative. This is the chief reason why there is no magazine comparable to *Twen* specifically geared to the lower class. At twenty or twenty-five lower-class people are married, or if not they ought to be, and once married they have

friends or marriage partners from among the inhabitants of their block of flats or part of the town. But readers of *Twen* are again encouraged to adopt a pioneering role. A girl living in Frankfurt who goes in for the 'Rendezvous 68' scheme is certain not to get a partner in Frankfurt, although she is equally certain not to get one in Hamburg or Munich. The reason is that although the latter are too far away for it to be possible to arrange a date, Frankfurt is too 'near'. The girl is much more likely to get the address of a boy in Mainz, Wiesbaden or Darmstadt – the author has tested this personally.

to bow to the general standard of consumption reigning outside the *Twen* frivolity market.

3. *The lower the social stratum, the higher must be the social and sexual ideal presented to its members, i.e. the more exalted must be the norm representing 'happiness' to them.*

This reciprocal relationship between ideal status and real status is demonstrated most simply by a comparison of magazines from the Springer Press, since these give the clearest picture of the spectrum of manipulation:

Table 3

| Magazine | Chiefly intended for | Ideal Status |
| --- | --- | --- |
| *Eltern* | Young middle-class wives, not especially ambitious | Outstanding examples of their own class, but always its top economic level; the childhood of successful politicians and other great men |
| *Twen* | Young unmarried adults, middle-class, with ambitions to join a social élite, and to go up in the world financially | Successful or attractively unconventional examples of their own class or the one higher (architects, sales promoters, models, weekend hippies) |
| *Bravo* | Young people from the lower class and the lower middle class | Pop singers, film stars, but chiefly those with close connexions to the working class: Roy Black, Pierre Briece, etc. |
| *Das Neue Blatt* | Chiefly resigned and isolated married couples from the lower social classes | Royalty |
| *Hör Zu* | Not specific | Film stars in general |

'Chiefly intended for' does not automatically mean 'read chiefly by'. For example, up to 38 per cent of *Bravo*'s readers are over thirty, and quite a number of middle-class and upper-class young people also read it. But the 'identification value' is not likely to be so high in their case; for example, adult men are likely to flip through *Bravo* for the pin-ups, and upper-class young people are scarcely likely to consult Dr Vollmer, or read an article about a pop singer's family background and friendship with his younger brother, with the same degree of identification as lower-class people.

This comparison of actual and ideal status is a good empirical guide to the way in which the gap widens between real and illusory needs, and between real needs and the possibility of their satisfaction, as one goes down the social and economic scale. The only examples of their own class and its way of life that lower-class people see in magazines are the heroes and the lucky: lottery winners, or people like the master mechanic who loved his wife so much that he worked for years in his spare time to make an artificial kidney to keep her alive.[11]

It is not unusual for *Das Neue Blatt* to run stories about the private lives of members of three European royal families, and in each case to make a particular point of how kind, respectful and considerate the young monarch is to the queen mother – a situation which old people encounter less and less frequently in our society, particularly in the lower class. The stars, the consorts of royalty, the kings and champion sportsmen, have the function which demi-gods had in mythology: they are human to a superlative degree, and therefore to be imitated; their behaviour has a normative character. But as they are not of this world, one can only imitate them in a small way, on one's own level, and not presume to match oneself with them in reality. Manipulation has the challenging task of maintaining identification with these demi-gods on an 'unreal' level, so that the manipulated are never struck by such ideas as: 'But what a stupid way to go on' – or 'It's impossible for me to get that high anyway, the same laws don't apply' – or 'To have that kind of family life you need to have money.' In principle this balance of identification also applies to classes and groups being manipulated through a status ideal located within their own social level or one near enough for them to think they can reach it.[12]

[11] Naturally the pressure to increase consumption stands in the foreground of this type of class-oriented manipulation as well. The readers of *Das Neue Blatt* are 'chiefly those attempting to climb the social scale, and people who are socially isolated'. Neither group has 'any very marked class sense'. According to the 1962 survey from which these observations are taken 'good sense makes *Das Neue Blatt* readers less on the look-out for something that is cheap than for something that is a bargain, on the principle that "you don't get something for nothing" '. Discovery of a particularly good source of bargains is experienced not only as a financial gain, but as a personal triumph. The magazine's 'Bargain Notes' help to prop up the insecure identities of its readers.

[12] As early as 1944 Horkheimer and Adorno drew attention to this principle of class-differentiated manipulation in their *Dialektik der Aufklärung*: 'Sharp differences such as exist between A and B films or the stories in high- and low-priced magazines do not simply arise from the nature of the subject matter, but are there to stratify, organize and dominate the consumers. The differences are worked out with the utmost precision, and spread to cover all possible types, so that no one can slip through the net.' (p. 147).

4. *Class manipulation of this kind produces an apparent 'equalizing' effect within the social structure. The price paid for this is a permanently restrictive situation in which needs are aroused by false sexualization which cannot be satisfied, leaving the manipulated in a perpetual state of disappointment.*

The 'universality' of sexual and other satisfactions has initially produced a strong pseudo-democratic effect. The culture industry has taken a step forward. Horkheimer and Adorno illustrate the point: 'The step from telephone to radio was a visible watershed. The telephone was a liberal form of communication in that it allowed every user to transmit his own programme; the radio democratically reduced everyone to the role of listeners, in order to submit them autocratically to the same or similar programmes and stations.'[13] 'Everyone' today has a car and a superfluity of clothes, and children all get the same pocket-money. Only by looking very carefully, and sometimes not even then, unless one is in the clothing business, or a fashion fetishist, can one tell the difference between a suit from a man's boutique of the Italian/American sort, an analogous suit from a chain store, and a suit from an old-fashioned gentleman's tailors.

Objects put up for exchange in the sphere of purchasable goods – just like those in the field of sexuality – have been robbed of their specificity. People are genuinely dissatisfied, but no longer with the specific attributes of the things they can get, or with the absence of the things they would like to get; indeed the dissatisfaction is all but covered by a deep layer of ostensible satisfaction brought about by a continuous increase in the purchase of goods, and the pursuit of ultimately unobtainable sexual objects. False needs can be created to infinity, and the boundaries of potential satisfaction grow with them. This develops an attitude of striving towards ever greater satisfaction, which dooms the individual to a state identical in its essentials to that of the sexual pervert who is forever stuck at a preparatory stage of the sex act, and thus remains perpetually frustrated.[14] The compulsive drive towards ever greater achievement that is brought about in our society by this collective perversion is one of the most vital factors in the functioning of the system, but it is becoming increasingly difficult, if not impossible, to investigate, because of the institutionalized coupling of dissatisfaction and illusory satisfaction.

[13] Horkheimer and Adorno: op. cit., p. 146.
[14] This question is examined in the section 'Narcissism and the genital façade' (see page 89 below).

These difficulties did not exist in the earlier stages of class society. Anyone denied access to the means of production could easily see that in order to obtain satisfaction for himself, he needed to take this source of satisfaction away from another (namely, the one who took it away from him in the first place: the exploiter). 'Taking it away won't do much good' is what the individual caught up in the vicious circle of dissatisfaction and false satisfaction seems to be saying – 'One's never satisfied anyhow.' Greater equality, real and illusory, in the world of consumer goods and of sexuality exists side by side with real differences in the level of satisfaction possible, making it ever more difficult to develop political conflicts out of social and economic differences, and thus sow the seeds of class struggle. This result could not have been obtained without the isolation of individuals that is brought about through manipulation and pressure to achieve and conform. Individuals have become so 'alike' that they are no longer able to recognize class differences, and are all competing with each other, for want of anything better, for the biggest share of manipulated satisfaction, in a spirit of 'myself versus the rest'.

Expressed in political terms, this represents a shift from collective social conflict (i.e. class conflict) to individual competition. It has long been established in socialist discussion that class lines have become ideologically blurred in late capitalist societies. This trend might, it has been suggested, be only a superficial political shift, a displacement of the class struggle, a closing of the ranks resulting from the projection of social and political conflicts onto an external enemy (Communism). This is not the case. If it were, the situation would be liable to change with changes in the world political situation. It is hoped that this chapter will have made clear some of the real origins of this change. They all have the purpose of hiding the structure of the life we live, and presenting it as unchangeable. As the different sectors of the population of advanced capitalist nations grow closer to each other *economically*, they are kept apart from each other by artificially created *social* differences. At the same time they are collectively prevented from building up an independent ego, and natural resources are harnessed not for the improvement of civilization, but for its destruction. Under such circumstances domination is omnipresent and faceless.

# Chapter 4

# The Repressive Conquest of Modern Nervous Illness

Starting from the study of mentally and sexually disturbed individuals, psycho-analysis demonstrated, for the first time, 'that in Man the sexual instinct does not originally serve the purposes of reproduction at all, but has as its aim the gaining of particular kinds of pleasure'.[1] In treating people who were incapable of full heterosexual intercourse, or who would not accept this manifestation of the sexual urge – either on moral grounds (abstinence) or because they were drawn to other so-called perverted or homosexual manifestations, and who suffered accordingly because of it – Freud found himself forced to inquire into the *sexual* reasons for these people's fate. He observed them, investigated them (analysis) and came to the conclusion that the sexual urge is very much present in childhood, but that it is not yet centred at that age on heterosexual intercourse with another person, but for the time being is *'without an object, auto-erotic'*.

Satisfaction arises first and foremost from the appropriate sensory excitation of what we have described as erotogenic zones. It seems probable that any part of the skin and any sense-organ – probably, indeed, *any* organ – can function as an erotogenic zone, though there are some particularly marked erotogenic zones, whose excitation would seem to be secured from the very first by certain organic contrivances. It further appears that sexual excitation arises as a by-product, as it were, of a large number of processes that occur in the organism, as soon as they reach a certain degree of intensity, and most especially of a relatively powerful emotion, even though it is of a distressing nature. The excitations from all these sources are not yet combined, but each follows its own separate aim, which is merely the attainment of a certain sort of pleasure. In childhood, therefore, the sexual instinct is not unified, and is at first *without an object*, that is *auto-erotic*.[2]

[1] Freud: *'Civilized' Sexual Morality and Modern Nervous Illness*, 1908, op. cit., vol. IX, p. 188.
[2] Freud: *Three Essays on Sexuality*, 1905, op. cit., vol. VII, pp. 232–3.

No further organic development takes place in sexual activity; rather, it is guided into specific directions and forms of expression by influences from the culture in which the child is born, chiefly the people in the family circle with whom the child is most closely connected. A decisive stage in the 'guiding' process is the Oedipal conflict, in the course of which the child must learn, (i) to completely give up desiring people of its own sex (redirection of instincts); (ii) to give up for the time being desiring people of the opposite sex (postponement of instincts); (iii) to permanently renounce sexual desire for mother and father (incest ban). These achievements lay the foundation for a whole number of important social and individual faculties, the majority of which are counted essential in any societies with a moderately complex system of production, communication, and need-gratification. An adequate resolution of the Oedipus complex (that is to say, one which lays the foundations for cultural development) must however build upon a number of already acquired faculties, which will have been established in various manifestations and forms of integration of the partial drives in the preceding phases (oral, anal, and phallic).

It would be confusing and incorrect to say at the end of the Oedipal phase infantile sexuality has been subjugated or blocked. If it has been, this indicates that the Oedipus complex has not been properly resolved, often because of the unsatisfactory resolution of earlier stages, and the certain result will be pathological developments in character and sexuality later on in childhood and adult life. It is equally false to see the Oedipus complex, and the phases preceding and following, as a process of sexual development alone. It would be a much more accurate description to say that every biological stage is ideally accompanied by the development of certain faculties, the sum total of which is referred to as ego-integration. Thus the resolution of the oral phase is accompanied by acquiring the cognitive faculty of distinguishing between the self and others, and by the first steps towards physiological control and integration of muscular activity. The anal, phallic, and Oedipal sexual phases are accompanied by a quasi-systematic further development of corresponding cognitive and physiological capacities.

Talcott Parsons was the first to describe this development process in terms of a sociological model of the socialization process.[3] Parsons however denies the independence of biological/

[3] Talcott Parsons: *Social Structure and Personality*, New York, 1964, in particular the chapter 'Social Structure and the Development of the Personality – Freud's Contribution to the Integration of Psychology and Sociology'.

libidinous aims (component instincts and erotogenic zones), so his sociological model tends towards total conformity with the existing social norms. His work does however have the undeniable distinction of having provided the psychoanalytic assessment of development in early childhood with a systematic sociological explanation. One must however guard against the mistake (made not only by Parsons but by other, more critical sociologists) of denying the basic biological determination of these early phases, described by Freud as sexual. Freud never entertained any doubt as to the biological reality of these phases and later empirical research has supported all his statements. They are definitely not just 'generalized symbols'[4] but exist as facts, and are the only foundation for later sexual, cultural and character development.

In the so-called latency period, which follows the end of the Oedipus complex and lasts until puberty, there is, according to Freud's interpretation, no break in the production of sexual energy; it is simply 'used chiefly for non-sexual purposes':

During the latency period the production of sexual excitation is not by any means stopped, but continues and produces a store of energy which is employed to a great extent for purposes other than sexual – namely, on the one hand, in contributing the sexual components to social feelings, and on the other hand (through repression and reaction-forming) in building up the subsequently developed barriers against sexuality. On this view, the forces destined to retain the sexual instinct upon certain lines are built up in childhood, chiefly at the cost of perverse sexual impulses and with the assistance of education. A certain portion of the infantile sexual impulses would seem to evade these uses and succeed in expressing itself as sexual activity.[5]

In puberty the sexual urge finally centres on heterosexual goals. Freud considers that the two most important changes connected with puberty are:

... The subordination of all the other sources of sexual excitation under the primacy of the genital zones and the process of finding an object. Both of these are already adumbrated in childhood. The first is accomplished by the mechanism of exploiting fore-pleasure: what were formerly self-contained sexual acts, attended by pleasure and excitation, become acts preparatory to the new sexual aim (the discharge of the sexual products) the attainment of which, enormously pleasurable, brings the sexual excitation to an end. ... As regards object-choice, we found that it is given its direction by the childhood

[4] Unlike Parsons's 'sociological' categories, which could be described as such.
[5] Freud: *Three Essays on Sexuality*, op. cit., p. 232.

hints (revived at puberty) of the child's sexual inclination towards his parents and others in charge of him, but that it is diverted away from them, on to other people who resemble them, owing to the barrier against incest which has meanwhile been erected. Finally it must be added that during the transition period of puberty the processes of somatic and psychical development continue for a time side by side independently, until the irruption of an intense mental erotic impulse, leading to the innervation of the genitals, brings about the unity of the erotic function which is necessary for normality.

Every step on this long path of development can become a point of fixation, every juncture in this involved combination can be an occasion for a dissociation of the sexual instinct, as we have already shown from numerous instances.[6]

Two points need particular stress:

1. The component instincts are not rejected in fully developed genital sexuality, but simply 'subordinated'. Even 'subordination' is too negative a term, in that it lays too much stress on the repressive side of a process which should ideally be the *integration* of the component instincts into the pattern of sexual development. It is perfectly possible to envisage that a person might develop to a fully genital state and be capable of complete sexual enjoyment by a process involving only non-repressive integration of the component instincts. A 'genital' character exists, corresponding to the genital state, in which a balance between control and acceptance of the instincts renders the individual capable of both achieving *and* enjoying, of being active *and* controlling himself, of concentrating his spiritual energy *and* being spontaneous. The specific strength of all these qualities, or sometimes the relative feebleness of one in relation to its obverse, determines the character structure of an individual. It *also* determines the degree to which he is subordinated to the ruling reality principle (conformity), flees from it or compulsorily obeys it (neurosis), or challenges and criticizes it (capacity for coping with reality). The people in any society, but particularly ours, who rigidly and compulsively fulfil the genital norms cannot properly be described as genital characters. Their social and sexual behaviour indicates that they have never attained a full genital structure. They are at once too weak to fulfil the social norms and too weak to refuse them, with the result that they have to forcibly prevent their unintegrated component instincts from showing themselves, and therefore put up a façade of genital behaviour.

[6] Freud: *Three Essays on Sexuality*, op. cit., pp. 234–5.

2. 'Every step on this long path of development can ... be an occasion for a dissociation of the sexual instinct.' In the following section we propose to discuss the various forms of dissociation typical of our culture, to discuss how they arise in social and individual cases in terms of the currently dominant reality principle, and so arrive at a formulation of the sexual type that is most prevalent today: the type of personality that compulsively fulfils the genital norms without having a basically genital psyche, the person with a genital façade.

Freud divided dissociation of the sexual instinct into 'two kinds of harmful deviation from normal sexuality, that is, sexuality which is serviceable to civilization', the relation between which 'is almost that of positive and negative'.[7] These are: *neuroses* (the structure of psychoses still renders them, as it did in Freud's day, more or less inaccessible to the methods of psycho-analysis) and *perversions* (in which 'an infantile fixation to a preliminary sexual aim has prevented the primacy of the reproductive function from being established'), together with the structurally different *homosexuality* (in which 'the sexual aim has been deflected away from the opposite sex'). The larger majority of neurotics and perverts are so only in relation to their culture. They either will not or cannot live up to its demands. Though *neurotics* have repressed all socially forbidden manifestations of the sex instincts in their lives, and quite often the socially permitted manifestations as well, this does not mean they have got rid of them, and the repressed urges return in an apparently non-sexual form, which is none the less fed by repressed sexuality. The *perverts* are, subjectively, somewhat better off than the neurotics. They have repressed too few components of the 'polymorphous perverted' (original) sexual instinct, and have thus never been able to organize the instinct into a genital heterosexual object choice. Or else they have regressed, after a period of initial and usually only apparent genital heterosexuality, to a manifestly infantile stage. When an individual becomes fixated at a certain stage, and does not develop further, regression has become 'dissociation of the sexual instinct'.

This does not imply, by any means, that all individuals who behave in perverted ways do without 'end-pleasure', the resolution of sexual tension in genitally produced orgasm. But for perverts orgasm plays a subordinate role, or it is produced by infantile practices which are basically those of 'fore-pleasure',

[7] Freud: *'Civilized' Sexual Morality and Modern Nervous Illness*, p. 189.

and are something quite separate from end-pleasure. Freud has summarized the differences and similarities between neuroses and perverions thus:

Where the sexual instinct is fairly intense, but perverse, there are two possible outcomes. The first, which we shall not discuss further, is that the person affected remains a pervert and has to put up with the consequences of his deviation from the standard of civilization. The second is far more interesting. It is that, under the influence of education and social demands, a suppression of the perverse instincts is indeed achieved, but it is a kind of suppression which is really no suppression at all. It can better be described as a suppression that has failed. The inhibited sexual instincts are, it is true, no longer expressed as such – and this constitutes the success of the process – but they find expression in other ways which are quite as injurious to the subject and make him quite as useless for society as satisfaction of the suppressed instincts in an unmodified form would have done. This constitutes the failure of the process, which in the long run more than counterbalances its success. The substitutive phenomena which emerge in consequence of the suppression of the instinct amount to what we call nervous illness, or, more precisely, the psychoneuroses. Neurotics are the class of people who, since they possess a recalcitrant organization, only succeed in achieving a suppression of their instincts which is *apparent* and which becomes increasingly unsuccessful. They therefore only carry on their collaboration with cultural activities by a great expenditure of force and at the cost of an internal impoverishment, or are obliged at times to interrupt it and fall ill. I have described the neuroses as the 'negative' of the perversions because in the neuroses the perverse impulses, after being repressed, manifest themselves from the unconscious part of the mind – because the neuroses contain the same tendencies, though in a stage of 'repression' as do the positive perversions.[8]

Freud assumed that in all social organization there was a proportional relationship between the level of cultural development (the degree of social differentiation, and the level of cultural and productive achievement) and the degree to which society needed to repress the instincts in order to maintain this achievement. In his theoretical writings Freud does not come down on the side of either 'civilization' or 'instinct'; he simply describes their antagonistic relationship and repeatedly comes to the conclusion that an inordinately high price in terms of oppression and sickness often has to be paid for the maintenance of society. The conclusion that the price is too high is not established on the basis of ethical standards from outside the sphere of pyscho-analysis, but by looking at the profits and losses

[8] Freud: *'Civilized' Sexual Morality and Modern Nervous Illness*, pp. 190–1.

on the civilization/instinct balance sheet. Neurotic individuals can 'only carry on their collaboration with cultural activities by a great expenditure of force and at the cost of an internal impoverishment, or are obliged at times to interrupt it and fall ill'.

I must insist upon the view that neuroses, whatever their extent and whenever they occur, always succeed in frustrating the purposes of civilization, and in that way actually perform the work of the suppressed mental forces that are hostile to civilization. Thus, when society pays for obedience to its far-reaching regulations by an increase in nervous illness, it cannot claim to have purchased a gain at all.[9]

In his work *'Civilized' Sexual Morality and Modern Nervous Illness* Freud developed a model of cultural development based upon the sexual development of the individual, emphasizing this theory that the repression of the instincts in a society increases according to the degree of civilization. The last of the stages described by Freud looks at first sight like the utmost manifestation of 'the repressive function of sexuality':

If this evolution of the sexual instinct is borne in mind, three stages of civilization can be distinguished: a first one in which the sexual instinct may be freely exercised, without regard to the aims of reproduction; a second, in which all of the sexual instinct is suppressed except what serves the aims of reproduction; and a third, in which only *legitimate* reproduction is allowed as a sexual aim. The third stage is reflected in our present-day 'civilized' sexual morality.[10]

This model contradicts all anthropological evidence that could be used to form a history of sexuality in civilization – including anthropological discoveries reported on by Freud himself.[11] What he is in fact doing in this passage is implicitly equating 'civilization' with a concept of *genital culture*, fully mature in the physical, psychological and social respects, and which would yet allow the possibility of enjoying sexual liberty over and above the needs of procreation. Much more straightforwardly illuminating is Freud's almost casual observation that 'oral' can be compared to 'cannibalistic'. This would mean that a certain type of character (oral) corresponds to a certain type of social organization (primitive, stationary, cannibalistic, etc.). According to this view genital sexuality would not be a purely

[9] op. cit., pp. 202–3.
[10] op. cit., p. 189.
[11] For instance, in *Totem and Taboo*, 1913 (Routledge paperback, 1960).

personal quality, which would occur irrespective of cultural, social and economic level. Rather, the genital character could only develop in economies with a comparatively complex division of labour in their mode of production, and whose social organization made high demands on the function of the individual ego. Components of this function would be: conscious understanding of social and technical processes, ability to reason in depth and exercise control over the social organization, acquisition and maintenance of performance standards, capacity for control of the instincts and sublimation.

Freud's negligence in this instance is all the more striking since he himself often states that the individual in his own development (ontogenesis) has to catch up on everything that his culture has achieved before him (phylogenesis) in speeded-up motion, with the exception of the small portion which he will have inherited directly. This would inevitably lead to the conclusion that there would be, corresponding to the pregenital stages of individual sexual development, pregenital historical (phylogenetic) eras in the collective sexual development of cultures. In reality the first two 'stages' (supposing that this means stages in pre-bourgeois society) were far from presenting a situation in which sexual liberty could be enjoyed over and above the needs of procreation. *Freedom* did not yet exist, in the sense of being free to organize one's own consciousness within the social situations; genital primacy had not yet been achieved. The chief reason why Freud did not see this was doubtless because he remained completely bound in his thought to bourgeois culture and all his historical models – including the very ancient one of patricide – were conceived in the categories of bourgeois culture.

'Modern nervous illness' is the collective sickness of the era which Freud analysed and described; it corresponds to his 'third stage of civilization'. In it, a large number of individuals suffer to such a degree under the sexual morality imposed upon them that the cultural purposes which their sufferings are supposed to serve are themselves endangered. Too many individuals become ill and have to 'interrupt their collaboration with cultural activities' because of the strain of fulfilling cultural norms and tasks. Naturally there were time-honoured methods of avoiding or masking actual neurotic illness, as for instance, the double moral standard in sexual matters for the male, and the female refusal of sex, or flight into religiosity or good works. But not only were these ways of avoiding neurosis somewhat neurotic in themselves – a disadvantage that could have been tolerated in the interests of society – but they became increasingly undesirable in the face of economic development and the corresponding repressive form of social organization in which the precise regulation of the functioning of each individual becomes very important. The change which has consequently taken place was outlined above with the example of rigid functionalism. Rigid sexual restraints are no longer necessary today in order to keep society going; indeed, the preservation of capitalist relations actually requires a 'relaxation' of the sexual morality which caused individual neuroses (collectively, 'modern nervous illness'). We still have neuroses, but now we have, existing alongside them, an ever increasing amount of other forms of cultural sickness.

The 'perverts' of Freud's epoch, now on the decline, were, to put the matter in somewhat ideal terms, those who had refused total acquiescence to the restraints of their culture and its sexual morality. They were rewarded for their resistance. Freud not infrequently speaks about them as though they were the heroes of their civilization. If they manage not to become the slaves of their perversions he feels able to pronounce them 'healthy, but from a social point of view immoral to an undesirable degree'.[12] This evaluation of course only applies to the type of pervert who has not only risen above the sexual morality of his culture and its neurotic manifestations, but has also to a certain degree achieved mastery of his own perversion, and remains capable of dealing with reality.

The average pervert however is unable to bear reality, or to enter into a constructive dialogue with it. Early in life he did not learn to control his instincts, and this inability continues into adulthood. Significantly, psychotic breakdowns in adult life, but most particularly in adolescence, as well as the various forms of schizophrenia and paranoia, have a similar background. The problem, formulated in very schematic and abbreviated terms, is that these individuals were insufficiently socialized by their early family situation. They had no unified models to follow in learning how to master and select their instincts, or to exercise the various types of self-control. Later in life the outside world (profession, school, peer group or adolescent boy-friend or girl-friend) 'suddenly' forces them in all too violent a manner to try and assume these qualities. Psychologically and socially, they are at a loss. They are not up to the demands which reality suddenly thrusts upon them, and endeavour to compen-

---

[12] Freud: *'Civilized' Sexual Morality and Modern Nervous Illness*, p. 192.

sate by going back to the earliest and most primitive methods of defending themselves against instinctual urges. Psychotic break-downs are only the most conspicuous manifestation of the various forms of abnormal behaviour that range from open perversion to clinical psychosis. They occur with significant frequency in children and young people from families with manifestly incestuous parent/child relationships, families with pathologically solicitous mothers (but where the solicitude is inconsistent), or from families in which the mother and father compete with each other in offering the child extremely contra-dictory and irreconcilable models with which to identify. The child is not equipped with the qualities that would enable it later to control reality (unified identification and object-choice, development and stabilization of the ego-functions, etc.). All these socialization processes resulting in perversion and psychosis seem to derive from a wrong development in extremely early childhood, long *before* the Oedipal phase, namely, at the oral and anal stages of pleasure, identification, object-love and ego-development.

If Freud's stages of civilization correspond by and large to different social and individual modes of gratification, then the first could be most closely related to feudalism, the second to the transition from feudalism to capitalism, and the third to puri-tanical capitalism. If we use these categories, we could say that today a 'fourth stage' had been reached in which the morality which allowed 'only *legitimate* reproduction' as a sexual aim is now relaxing somewhat. But this relaxation is not identical with freedom 'without regard to the aims of reproduction', but is regression to a stage even beneath that of the compulsive adoption of the outward appearances of genital sexuality. In historical terms, one might call it collective dissociation (disso-lution) of the genital structure of the the sexual instinct. The individual no longer reaches the stage in which his instinctual urges are organized into a genital structure, or at best only reaches it in part. In particular the process of moving on from auto-eroticism to object-love has become more difficult, as has that by which the different erotogenic zones, after previously functioning as separate entities, become unified under a conscious apparatus focusing libidinous desires onto outside objectives. This is because the necessary socialization processes are growing more and more feeble, or even no longer taking place at all. In any case, very strong counter-tendencies start to act on the child earlier and last longer. The individual and col-lective social character and sexual practice resulting from this phenomenon bear a strong resemblance to those characteristic of psychosis.

## PERPETUAL PUBERTY AND FREE-FLOATING SEXUALITY

The 'manipulative equalization' studied in the last chapter rests chiefly upon three psychological phenomena: (i) the fetishization of the objects consumed (whether sexually or really), (ii) by indifference to the objects themselves and lack of differentiation between them, and (iii) an unspecific but ever growing fear of losing them.[13] This fear appears to be the active component of this 'manipulation equalization' and seems capable of dividing society's members from each other to eternity.

These phenomena point back to a stage in the development of the individual in which fear and lack of discrimination in object-choice are predominant qualities: early childhood. Young children are extremely dependent and in need of protection. This is a natural phenomenon in the human species, which needs an unusually long time, in comparison with the animal world, to reach autonomous maturity, but it is the aim of education to overcome the child's dependence and make it into a relatively self-sufficient adult. Young children are not only dependent, they are by nature perfectly egoistic and unsocial; they only love what gives them pleasure, without regard to what it is. They are, as Freud said, auto-erotic to a high degree. The child also has widely varied sources of auto-erotic pleasure (erotogenic zones). Of course he quickly has to learn that it is not always he himself who is providing the gratification (the paradigm being that the breast which gives him pleasure is his mother's), that other people provide it for him, and that he is dependent on them. The growth of independence coincides with the beginnings of an ego (consciousness). Subsequently his dependence is overcome through growing-achievement. *How* this happens will be a decisive factor in his future psychological health.

However, while this process of education into independence is taking place within in the family, counter processes are also working on the child from outside, though in a disguised form, and using the influence of the family itself. The purpose of these

[13] This aspect has been particularly clearly described by W. F. Haug in *Das Argument*, 1964: 'Waren-Ästhetik und Angst' ('Anxiety and the Aesthetics of Consumption'). '... how manipulative advertising works: it sets the standards of what is "lovable" and so manipulates the latent fear of loss of love.'

is to keep him in a state of dependence so that he can be controlled and manipulated. The fact that people become independent of their families earlier today sheds light on this process rather than contradicts it. It is indicative that the family is ceasing to play its classic role, more especially when this 'independence' is not the genuine result of education given within the family, but represents the victory of external educative influences working against it, and especially when the individual's independence of his family is really increased dependence on other sources of authority.

When this happens, it means that the young person has not achieved the transformation into adulthood which was the classic goal of puberty, but is held back in *perpetual puberty*. We have described puberty as the stage during which, in Freud's terms, 'all other sources of sexual excitation (are subordinated) under the primacy of the genital zones and the process of finding an object'. The object to be found is by definition of the opposite sex, and outside the family (avoidance of incest). In our culture, the attachment is intended to be unique and binding. Genital primacy and the corresponding formation of a mature object-love can however only come about if the love/hate relationship characteristic of the child's *identification* with its parents in the latency period is resolved, i.e. if the son or daughter can build up a state of self-sufficiency through constructive conflict with its parents. External barriers against this appear to have weakened in recent years, because of the loss of parental authority caused by historic and economic circumstances. This is especially so in Germany, due to fascism.

The internal obstacles have however become more severe. In *Die Unfähigkeit zu Trauern* A. and M. Mitscherlich comment that 'the decrease in effective paternal authority within the family has given the child a better possibility of working out its Oedipal conflicts openly than it had before. But the result of this process is not only greater freedom, but also sometimes a greater lack of direction, because the object (father or mother) against whom open protest was previously directed is not now such a ready target for aggression.' This is so because he or she has less real power. Young people can still fight their parents, argue with their views, but they cannot use them as a springboard for a leap into independence. In this situation, both fathers and sons regress to the same infantile stage. 'Both fathers and sons [say the Mitscherlichs] seem to be searching for a "father" – a super-father – yet to have ambivalent feelings towards him, and not be very ready to recognize him as an ideal.'

The fact that external circumstances have made it easier to break away does not make it easier for young people to take on the 'parental' role of assuming responsibility, becoming self-sufficient adults, and learning how to love. They have the added difficulty that the enfeebled parental authority has been replaced by enormously strong sources of authority stemming from outside the family. It is difficult for them to stand up to this sort of authority because it cannot be pinned down to a person, and because they have not in any case learned how to *resist*; their family was an unsatisfactory practice ground. The typical result is that they never do resolve the situation, but continue in the pre-Oedipal stage of ambivalent identification. The Mitscherlichs characterize the situation in this way: 'They do not protest, but they are not "well behaved" either. They remind one of the orphans described by Anna Freud, whose normal pattern of emotional ties to their mother was cut off early by her death, after which no substitute was forthcoming. These children have a comparatively normal development in childhood, but then suffer severe disturbances in puberty.'

There is of course no doubt that the new agencies of socialization outside the family also assume the class transformations of puberty as their stated or unstated norm. But they go about it in such a way that the individual is always unsuccessfully searching for an object for his love, and is always in a state of sexual tension which it is impossible to relieve. Freud used a striking and beautiful image to describe the 'transformations of puberty':

A normal sex life is only assured by an exact convergence of the affectionate current and the sensual current, both being directed towards the sexual object and sexual aim. (The former, the affectionate current, comprises what remains over of the infantile efflorescence of sexuality.) It is like the completion of a tunnel which has been driven through a hill from both directions.[14]

It appears as though it were the stated aim of the new social sources of authority to dig wildly from both sides but in directions calculated to just miss each other, so that young people never come up into daylight but have to remain forever in the darkness of fear, uncertainty and tension.

This contradiction is a basic element of all manipulative advertising, and the sexualization of films and newspapers, as well as the fashions, dances and music expressive of young people's new way of life. There is a perpetual incitement to buy an undifferentiated mass of sexual objects, which make their

[14] Freud: *Three Essays on Sexuality*, p. 207.

appeal to the uncoordinated component instincts; objects which one 'must have', which promise eternal gratification and pleasure, and yet which force the buyer to start looking around immediately for something more.

It used to be characteristic of adolescent love that the process of seeking someone or something to love was not at this stage fully developed, and that the young person very often proceeded on a 'narcissistic' principle in his love life. He fell passionately in love with all kinds of possible and impossible people, even veering between homosexuality and heterosexuality to an astonishing degree. It was generally agreed that these affairs were 'not serious' in so far as the adolescent was able to withdraw his admiration or veneration from a person or thing with a speed impossible to a mature adult, and endow another person or thing with it immediately afterwards. Anna Freud says about these love affairs:

These passionate and evanescent love-fixations are not object-relations at all in the sense in which we use the term in speaking of adults. They are identifications of the most primitive kind, such as we met with in our study of early infantile development, before any object-love exists. Thus the fickleness characteristic of puberty does not indicate any inner change in the love or convictions of the individual but rather a loss of personality in consequence of a change in identification.[15]

On the other hand, classic adolescent love affairs have a high degree of spontaneity and openness which older people's affairs – often so full of resignation and compromise – painfully lack.

The kind of love affairs we mean when we talk about 'perpetual puberty' have neither the mature steadfastness of adult relationships nor the overflowing openness of adolescent identification. The possibility of a firm love-relationship seems to be absent from the beginning. Nor do such relationships seem to possess a sufficient degree of the capacity for healthy auto-erotic (narcissistic) attachment to achieve the subjectively honest and emotionally overflowing passions typical of adolescence. These 'lovers' cannot get over puberty, chiefly for the reason that they lack the pre-pubic mental and emotional foundations needed for its development. If they do get so far as sexual intercourse they are bound to have transitory or permanent neurotic disturbances (as for instance vaginal anaesthesia in a woman) or else to take an equivalent perverted attitude to

<hr>

[15] Anna Freud: *The Ego and the Mechanisms of Defence*, London, 1948, pp. 185–6.

sexuality (as for instance Don Juanism – neurotic womanizing – in men).

Don Juanism – both in its old and new form – provides a most telling example of the socially conformist type of perversion, where the sufferer is neither abnormal, nor rebellious, nor noticeably sick (neurotic in the eyes of the community), nor actively perverted. In its psychoanalytic archetype, Don Juanism is a condition stemming from latent homosexuality. The sufferer's identification with his father was 'off balance'. If in later life he dashes from woman to woman, only loving and desiring them for a few days or even a few hours, and then, if they accede to his wishes, plunging them into unhappiness, 'in reality' it is his mother he is running after, and paying her back for the emotional violence she did him in the Oedipal stage, when he was so completely vanquished in the competition with his father that he could not even identify with his mother (which could have made open homosexuality possible). A frequent 'punishment' of the typical Don Juan is the neurotic symptom of impotence in erection or ejaculation, which constantly brings his own sickness to his attention, and from which he suffers. Oscar Wilde's Dorian Gray is a Don Juan and also 'perpetually pubescent' (he stays eternally young). We do not hear that he has any open neurotic symptoms, but he is addicted to opium, and finally has to murder the person who reveals to him the secret of his 'perpetual puberty'.

The contemporary forms of Don Juanism seem to escape 'punishment' through neurosis. On the contrary, under late capitalism there is an institutionalized system of Don Juanism, which has knit so tightly together that, in time, it will increasingly eliminate the traditional forms of cultural damage (neurotic illness which appears to the sufferer as neurotic). Up to now, this system has been considered in terms of authority granting broader sexual freedom. In fact, however, it is only the outer surface of a change which, for the second time in the history of capitalism, 'touches the very foundations of the social character'.[16] As time goes on this freedom will extend even more; it is ever more comprehensively propagated today. Young people's magazines are one indication, and there are even clearer signs in the USA, as we shall see.

This system is based, among other things, upon a loosening of object-relations, and a new course taken by socialization put-

---

[16] To quote Max Horkheimer's admirable definition. See 'Die Juden und Europa' in *Zeitschrift für Sozialforschung*, vol. VIII, Paris, 1939, p. 118.

ting firm object-relations completely out of the question. Looked at this way it would seem that the amount of neurotic illness and other kinds of subjectively experienced sexual conflict still occurring today is due on the one hand to the tenacity of the old capacity for forming object-relations, and on the other hand to the uneven development of different socialization institutions and the contradictions which consequently exist between them, which at the very best are bound to give young people a foretaste of the antagonistic contradictions of our society. Indeed we begin our political work by pointing out the contradictions in social institutions, whether the subject under discussion is automation in the factories, the feudal structure of the universities and the drying up of their financial resources, or the hostility of schools to sexuality.

## NARCISSISM AND THE GENITAL FAÇADE

The mechanisms and changes we have so far described are only a *tendency* in the sexual behaviour of our society. We are not yet in a position to say that people have become incapable of marrying, loving monogamously, begetting children and bringing them up, drawing a dividing line between their sex-life and their work, etc. Indeed society still encourages them to do so. But these faculties are losing the integrating context which they had in principle, even if not generally in *fact*, in bourgeois society. In its place a network of interrelated compulsions and limited possibilities for freedom is in operation. These are external, compartmentalized, and to a certain degree inorganic. Increased freedom can be used to justify increased compulsion. A simple example: if marriage now has an almost institutionalized permissiveness built into it towards 'harmless' or even 'necessary' extra-marital affairs, the social compulsion on which it is permanently based will become easier to bear, more legitimate, and more difficult to 'see through'. The 'new meaning of marriage' is a highly successful way of enforcing conformity. To gain insight into the controls used to cement this conformity, we need to study a few more of the mechanisms of the system related to those discussed in the last section.

*Narcissism* is not so absolutely identical to auto-eroticism as it might up till now have appeared. In fact it develops from it, at the same time as the ego develops out of the original infantile unity of ego and non-ego.[17] According to psycho-analysis, the

---

[17] Freud asks in *On Narcissism: An Introduction*: 'What is the relation of

child acquires two basic sexual objects in the course of ego-development: 'We say that a human being has originally two sexual objects – himself and the woman who nurses him – and in doing so we are postulating a primary narcissism in everyone, which may in some cases manifest itself in a dominating fashion in his object-choice.'[18] Freud analysed the child's relationship to its two original sexual objects and arrived at a definition of the two kinds of object-choice which can dominate in the attitudes of the child and the adult. He called the first the *anaclitic* or *attachment type*. This comprises all the kinds of relationship which I have categorized as object-relations (the classic case of this – anaclitic – dependence is the child's pleasure in being dependent on its mother); the second type Freud called *narcissistic object-choice* (love of oneself).[19] Both types build upon 'primary narcissism' meaning the libidinal centre from which desires and libidinous impulses are directed outwards (e.g. another person is 'loved'). In the second type these libidinous impulses are directed chiefly onto the person himself; behaviour of this type is consequently also known as 'secondary narcissism'.

Freud carried this distinction further, to describe the typically 'male' and 'female' types of object-choice. These applied not only to the 'well-to-do classes'[20] who were the only ones he analysed, but also to the general standards of sexual behaviour and choice of partner in capitalism and the power systems which preceded it:

A comparison of the male and female sexes then shows that there are fundamental differences between them in respect of their type of object-choice, although these differences are of course not universal.

---

narcissism . . . to auto-erotism? . . . We are bound to suppose that a unity comparable to the ego cannot exist in the individual from the start; the ego has to be developed. The auto-erotic instincts, however, are there from the very first; so there must be something added to auto-erotism – a new psychical action – in order to bring about narcissism.' (1914, op. cit., vol. XIV, pp. 76–7).

[18] Freud: op. cit., p. 88.

[19] op. cit. The division that Freud makes between these two types is based upon the division he makes between ego-instincts and sexual instincts, which he later abandoned in favour of the sexuality/destruction polarity. The distinction between the two types of object-choice is a correct one to make, however.

[20] Freud uses this formulation in an essay which reflects critically on the limited social field covered by psycho-analysis as a therapy: *Lines of Advance in Psycho-Analytic Therapy*, 1919, op. cit., vol. XVII, p. 166.

Complete object-love of the attachment type is, properly speaking, characteristic of the male. It displays marked sexual overvaluation which is doubtless derived from the child's original narcissism and thus corresponds to a transference of that narcissism to the sexual object. This sexual overvaluation is the origin of the peculiar state of being in love, a state suggestive of a neurotic compulsion which is thus traceable to an impoverishment of the ego as regards libido in favour of the love-object. A different course is followed in the type of female most frequently met with, which is probably the purest and truest one. With the onset of puberty the maturing of the female sexual organs, which up till then have been in a condition of latency, seems to bring about an intensification of the original narcissism, and this is un-favourable to the development of a true object-choice with its accompanying sexual overvaluation. Women, especially if they grow up with good looks, develop a certain self-contentment which compensates them for the social restrictions that are imposed upon them in their choice of object. Strictly speaking, it is only themselves that such women love with an intensity comparable to that of the man's love for them. Nor does their need lie in the direction of loving, but of being loved; and the man who fulfils this condition is the one who finds favour with them.[21]

This coordinates very well with the assumption that the types of object-choice produced by our society and most prevalent in it are coming to belong less and less exclusively to either the anaclitic, loving, category, or to the narcissistic category that desires to be loved. In fact both sexes – or to put it in more sociological terms, a greater number of individuals – are beginning to adopt a 'mixture' of both attitudes: they are kept in a state of narcissism like the bourgeois woman, without being able to compete with her 'self-contentment'. They love like the man, but without his 'power to remove repressions and re-instate perversions',[22] and they can reckon even less than he could on the chance of fulfilment of their 'state of being in love' by real love. For, taking the matter at its most extreme, there is no one left who is capable of love, only people who are seeking for a narcissistic extension of their own enfeebled egos.

The bourgeois male's 'state of being in love' described by Freud is characterized by an overflowing of the narcissistic (or ego-) libido onto the object, whereby the sexual object is elevated to a 'sexual ideal'. In contrast, the orientation towards narcissistic object-choice causes a person to love another because the other is 'what he once was and no longer is, or

[21] *On Narcissism: An Introduction*, pp. 88–9.
[22] op. cit., p. 100.

else possesses the excellences which he never had at all'.[23] In ideal circumstances 'the woman' did possess those excellencies and did not need to hunt frantically for an 'ego ideal', having found fulfilment in being loved. Freud thus makes a sharp division between loving and being loved; the first, consisting of 'longing and deprivation, lowers self-regard'; the second heightens self-regard, even when one does not 'really' love. Where the two coincide Freud qualifies the resulting state as 'real happy love'. One loves and is loved in return. He calls this a 'primal condition' (we should say 'utopian') 'in which object-libido and ego-libido cannot be distinguished'.[24]

In place of this 'real happy love' – which Freud thought of as a real, practical possibility – there are today an ever increasing number of new and unmistakably neurotic forms of 'being in love', which provide neither the strength to form object-relations, or to sustain a weakening of the ego (at the expense of libido), nor the self-contentment of a naturally narcissistic person. The idealized type of the 'bourgeois individual' had a firmly established base from which to send out his libido into the outside world, a *strong ego*. Family and society educated him and integrated him, with the result that he learnt to recon-cile the demands of his instincts (his id) with the outside world and with the moral and ethical norms of internalized culture (his super-ego), in this way he built up an ego for himself which always had a certain degree of strength. The person with a strong and autonomous ego has, besides his instinctual strength, also the capacity for postponing the gratification of his instincts (high tolerance of frustration) and for transforming them (sub-limation). When we talk about 'having a firmly established base for one's libido' or 'being able to form object-relations' or 'having reached a state of mature genital sexuality', we are basically talking about the same thing, the personality type described above. In the present day it seems to have undergone a permanent shift. But this is not the same as a general relaxa-tion of restraints on the instincts such as is suggested by the Mitscherlichs when they talk about the 'uncontrolled gratifica-tion' of young people today:

Uncontrolled gratification has the consequence of making the young person more amenable to manipulation. He enters upon sexual experi-ence before he is old enough to control it. The state proffered him in the guise of freedom is in fact one of early, unhealthy fixation. Sexu-ality is experienced as a remedy to an unhealthy state, and thus, strictly

[23] op. cit., p. 101.    [24] op. cit., pp. 99–100.

speaking, as nothing but self-gratification. No exchange of feelings, no entering into the other person's emotions is involved at all.[25]

We are in agreement with the Mitscherlichs about the result: socially encouraged perversion. But the gratification is far from being completely unbounded, it is fairly precisely channelled. The basis upon which this manipulated gratification works is what the Mitscherlichs describe as a 'weakness of the ego in the face of the instincts and social compulsions',[26] that is to say an ego which is insufficiently developed to mediate between id and super-ego plus outside world. The ego is subjected to violent assault 'from outside' by both instincts and social compulsions. The structure of these individuals' instincts has been insufficiently prepared for genital primacy. But it does not seem that they have become psychologically unhealthy because their instincts *and* their egos are not sufficiently controlled, but rather because their instincts *and* their egos are not sufficiently developed. (It should be stressed that an increase in the strength of the instincts does *not* imply a decrease in the strength of the ego). It seems as though these individuals have been 'purposely equipped with a feeble ego, and subsequently kept tractable, from adolescence on, by deliberate exercises in sexual 'relaxation'. One can of course only talk about a relaxation in sexual rules in comparison with historically antecedent states; ontologically, it is hardly the right word. It appears to connect with inadequate instinctual development; the individual has never learnt to unify his component instincts. It is impossible for me to say why this particular infantile phenomenon should connect with the equally infantile phenomenon of remaining, so far as the functioning of one's ego is concerned, in a state of weakness and dependence. But it is certain that these individuals show a tendency to break down under the genital primacy forced upon them by society, even if this is only a façade which is constantly under attack from pregenital instincts. They behave, though in a more socially conformist and less obvious way, very like Freud's perverts,[27] or the sex-offenders studied by the Kinsey group[28]

25 *Die Unfähigkeit zu Trauern*, p. 290.
26 op. cit., p. 286.
27 See Freud: '*A Child is being Beaten*': *A Contribution to the Study of the Origin of Sexual Perversions*, 1919, op. cit., vol. XVII, p. 192: 'For we find often enough with these perverts that they too made an attempt at developing normal sexual activity, usually at the age of puberty; but their attempt had not enough force in it and was abandoned in the face of the first obstacles which inevitably arise, whereupon they fell back upon their infantile fixation once and for all.'
28 See Gebhard and others: *Sex Offenders*, New York, 1965, p. 75: 'One

who began with attempts at normal heterosexual communication, but because of their basically infantile sexual attitude, reverted, when they met with the least resistance, to manifestly infantile forms of sexual gratification.

These pseudo-genital individuals find themselves obliged from a certain age on to prove that they are capable of functioning as genital characters in order to be accepted by the community, and so they adhere to conventional heterosexual practice (coitus or petting). But they are not properly equipped for this as they are incapable of object-choice. Their inner organization is infantile and narcissistic, but without the independence of the self-contented narcissist. Their organization is pregenital, and yet they carry on very active genital sex-relations with each other, often as if under compulsion. It remains an open question to what degree the term 'unhealthy' can be applied to this kind of behaviour. The sufferers do not give the impression of psychological degeneration and enslavement to instinct which characterizes some perverts; on the whole they are rather 'well-behaved' (to use Anna Freud's term). On thing is certain: that they share with many perverts the sexual characteristic of being unable to move beyond *fore-pleasure* to achieve sexual satisfaction in *end-pleasure*. Quite often without being aware of it, they are doomed to remain in a state of permanent sexual tension. What does this mean?

Psychoanalytic theory has formulated the insight, from the study of neurotic case-histories, that a state of sexual tension, in whatever circumstances it may appear or whatever may be its cause, is of necessity *unpleasant*. Because this is so, it motivates a 'change in the psychological situation'. The highest pleasure of all is orgasm; it is also the greatest release of energy. It is 'brought about entirely by discharge; it is wholly a pleasure of satisfaction and with it the tension of the libido is for the time being extinguished'.[29] This is the normal course of sexual

---

pedophile, who was sociosexually underdeveloped, had a case history which affords a simple story of the genesis of his pedophilia. As a child he had gratifying prepubertal sex play with girls, but in early postpubertal life he found his female peers had become much more difficult to deal with. The days of unashamed mutual exploration and play were ended, the girls were now aware of social demands, and had something of an adult attitude towards sex. The boy felt awkward and embarrassed with girls his own age, a typical early teenage situation, but unlike the typical teenager he responded by reverting to females of prepubertal age. This led to his first arrest.'

[29] Freud: *Three Essays on Sexuality*, p. 210. On p. 209 of the same work, Freud writes, about 'unpleasure': 'In spite of all the differences of opinion

gratification. Its mechanism is one of unpleasure leading to pleasure, and therein lies the difference between *fore-pleasure* and *end-pleasure*:

This distinction between the one kind of pleasure due to the excitation of erotogenic zones and the other kind due to the discharge of the sexual substance deserves, I think, to be made more concrete by a difference in nomenclature. The former may be suitably described as 'fore-pleasure' in contrast to the 'end-pleasure' or pleasure of satisfaction derived from the sexual act. Fore-pleasure is thus the same pleasure that has already been produced, although on a smaller scale, by the infantile sexual instinct; end-pleasure is something new and thus is probably conditioned by circumstances that do not arise till puberty. The formula for the new function of the erotogenic zones runs therefore: they are used to make possible, through the medium of the fore-pleasure which can be derived from them (as it was during infantile life), the production of the greater pleasure of satisfaction.[30]

It is certainly incorrect to think of the capacity for achieving end-pleasure as something mechanical, connected with the maturing of the sexual organs. This is certainly not what Freud meant when he connected it physiologically with the 'discharge of the sexual products'. The high rate of psychologically determined impotence in men, and incapability of experiencing orgasm in women, is conclusive proof that a physical ability to perform the act is simply a precondition for the experiencing of 'adult' orgasm but is far from being its be-all and end-all. Also end-pleasure itself varies in intensity under the influence of psychological factors. The manifest forms of genital insufficiency are only the most extreme case in a whole scale of experience leading from a complete incapacity for orgasm to total satisfaction. End-pleasure also varies in kind, and some of the states so qualified undoubtedly do not deserve the name. Nor, contrary to Wilhelm Reich's theories on the subject,[31] does full orgasm appear to be the prerogative of the classic genital union, or even

---

that reign on the subject among psychologists, I must insist that a feeling of tension necessarily involves unpleasure. What seems to me decisive is the fact that a feeling of this kind is accompanied by an impulsion to make a change in the psychological situation, that it operates in an urgent way which is wholly alien to the nature of the feeling of pleasure. If, however, the tension of sexual excitement is counted as an unpleasurable feeling, we are at once brought up against the fact that it is also undoubtedly felt as pleasurable. In every case in which tension is produced by sexual processes it is accompanied by pleasure.'
[30] Freud: op. cit., p. 210.
[31] At any rate, according to what seems the only possible interpretation of his *The Function of the Orgasm*, Panther edn, London, 1969.

of its heterosexual variants. Fore-pleasure is not identical with the 'preparatory sex-play' investigated by Kinsey, with a view to discovering how it varied in different social groups. He qualified it as the sexual activity leading up to the 'real' sex act, whether homo- or heterosexual, and measure its length, its quality, and the techniques employed. In our opinion it is much rather a part of the act itself, whatever the techniques employed. Certain possible techniques, which are considered part of preparatory sex-play, can become divided from genital sexuality, in the way that fore-pleasure is divided from end-pleasure. Where such a tendency occurs it is regressive and perverted. People with a genital façade cannot however properly be described as manifesting such tendencies. Their genital sexuality may be something false, and imposed from without, but they do practise it in the classic manner.

Freud in his era was of course only able to describe the 'genuine' type of perversion. In *Three Essays* he writes:

The connection between fore-pleasure and infantile sexual life is, however, made clearer by the pathogenic part which it can come to play. The attainment of the normal sexual aim can clearly be endangered by the mechanism in which fore-pleasure is involved. This danger arises if at any point in the preparatory sexual processes the fore-pleasure turns out to be too great and the element of tension too small. The motive for proceeding further with the sexual process then disappears, the whole path is cut short, and the preparatory act in question takes the place of the normal sexual aim. Experience has shown that the pre-condition for this damaging effect is that the erotogenic zone concerned or the corresponding component instinct shall already during childhood have contributed an unusual amount of pleasure. If further factors then come into play, tending to bring about a fixation, a compulsion may easily arise in later life which resists the incorporation of the particular fore-pleasure into a new context. Such is in fact the mechanism of many perversions, which consist in a lingering over the preparatory acts of the sexual process.[32]

The pseudo-genital type has not necessarily had 'an unusual amount of pleasure' from 'the corresponding component instinct' during childhood. There is no clinical evidence to support such an assumption. Nor is he an anal sadist, an underwear or shoe fetishist, or a pederast in the classic sense. He practises heterosexual intercourse which generally even results in orgasm. The pervert, as described by psycho-analysis, failed to resolve

[32] op. cit., p. 211.

his Oedipus complex because of pre-Oedipal experiences.[33] Thus the fetishist is constantly reminded by his fetish of the female penis, which, in his phallic or pre-phallic stage, he had refused to accept did not exist. He saw in the woman's lack of a penis a threat of castration, for her and for him. He is thus in need of a fetish which he can regard as a female penis in order to achieve 'some kind' of gratification. On condition of being able to imaginatively invest someone with his fetish, he can achieve strong dependence of another person, on the pre-Oedipal model.

The contemporary sexual type, the person with a genital façade, is a different case. He does live in a permanent fear of castration, as Peter Brückner confirmed in his observation of the sexual atmosphere of the 'hot summer' in Berlin. But he has to be permanently changing his fetish, and quite often, the person on whom he endows it as well. This, at any rate, is the conclusion we are bound to draw from observing the compulsive norms of direct and indirect sexual behaviour laid down for people by the agencies of manipulation, especially fashion. Manipulative fashion, which can no longer be equated with fashion in the classic sense, exemplifies the influences which prevent this type from getting beyond fore-pleasure. Not content with prescribing what modern man and his girl-friend should wear, which part of their body should be partially eroticized by the way they wear it (mini or maxi skirt), and suggesting that if they do not comply they will not be attractive, advertising also dictates complexion colour, hair colour, hair style (transforming the natural shape of the head) and a multitude of other special practices, ranging from the way in which one holds a whisky glass and the way one smokes a cigar or a cigarette, to how one dances, how one walks along the street, and how one goes to bed with somebody, which have to be adopted if attractiveness is to be kept at full market value.

All these accessories simultaneously reduce and fetishize personal attributes. If they fall out of favour, a complete reversal can occur from one day to the next. The type of person we are

---

[33] See Freud: *Fetishism*, 1927, op. cit., vol. XXI, p. 152: 'When I now announce that the fetish is a substitute for the penis, I shall certainly create disappointment; so I hasten to add that it is not a substitute for any chance penis, but for a particular and quite special penis that had been extremely important in early childhood but had later been lost. That is to say, it should normally have been given up, but the fetish is precisely designed to preserve it from extinction. To put it more plainly: the fetish is a substitute for the woman's (the mother's) penis. . . .'

discussing is not exactly perverted, since he changes his sexual object when advertising demands that he does so, and he unhesitatingly fulfils all heterosexual (or in special cases homosexual) norms. He is simply a highly variable fetishist. The rapidity with which he changes his fetish is ultimately a function of the rate of circulation of capital. Adorno and Horkheimer noted this more than twenty years ago in their *Dialektik der Aufklärung*. That this causation is in operation today is proved by the compulsive methods by which people are forced to adopt manipulative fashion, and by the very high rate of change in fashion itself.

# Chapter 5
# Examples of Late-capitalist
# Sexual Practice

In this chapter I should like to discuss one or two of the constrictive patterns currently imposed on sexuality. This book is not intended as a work of sexual enlightenment in the technical sense, nor should the descriptions of sexual practices which follow be read as studies of sexual technique (e.g. for maximization of pleasure, or birth control, or choice of husband or wife). Of course even works of that kind have – at least implicitly – a political and social content. The actual differences that exist today in the speech of different social groups, their comprehen-hension of economic events in the surrounding society, their capacity for rational thought, and not least in their attitudes to sexual practice, could lead one to the conclusion that perhaps even socially critical works of sexual enlightenment ought to be written today with particular classes in mind. Although this would be unjustified, it does not free us from the necessity of attempting the task, at times very difficult, of understanding the direction and mechanism of the techniques employed by the present system to ensure its continuance in power.

## PROMISCUITY AS THE COMPLETION OF MARRIAGE

In our society affective and sensual needs are very often, though not always, separated from each other. Monogamous marriage is by definition supposed to be based on a union of the two. And it is very probable that monogamous marriage today fulfils this condition better than the classic bourgeois (*not* petty-bourgeois) family studied and criticized by psycho-analysis, or the aristo-cratic family whose members felt, with the casual arrogance of a class securely in power, that they could dispense with such conditions in their own case if they wanted to. Sexual drives could only in rare and lucky circumstances find fulfilment in the predominantly economic institution of bourgeois marriage. Thrust out from society, they continued a protest existence of their own underground, in brothels and bohemia. As capitalism progressed, the continuing non-fulfilment of sexual drives by marriage became more absorbed into marriage itself, in the characteristic new form of semi-fulfilment. The role of the brothel was increasingly taken over by free-lance prostitution, which provides little more than quick and easy physical relief, and by the real increase in the possibilities for marital and pre-marital sexual gratification. In extreme cases the complete apparatus of the brothel has been taken over by marriage, and the conjugal bedroom may contain instruments and potions which a bourgeois at the end of the nineteenth century could only imagine existing behind the drapery in brothels and courtesans' boudoirs. Beate Uhse sends out the more respectable variety on a mass-produced scale, and semi-clandestine direct mail firms provide for more sadistic requirements.

By 'semi-fulfilment' I mean that though a very wide system of techniques is being employed to make people contented with their sexual lot (see the examples from *Eltern* in Chapter 3), they reach very tricky ground when it comes to marriage, because of the opposite tendency of maintaining people before marriage and during married life in a state of unfulfillable fore-pleasure. Now in the 'best years of their lives' people are supposed to make the best possible use of their situation, that is to say they should devote the best of their sexual selves to the enjoyment of marriage, but they are thwarted in this aim in an almost 'natural' way by the pictures of unattainable beauty, youth, freshness and success which are forever hovering before their eyes like vast advertisements, inciting them to perpetual imitation. A whole new branch of literature has developed to cope with the problems of adaptation this poses. In *Lifelong Happiness*, the catalogue of Beate Uhse's 'Mail-Order Service for Marriage Hygiene', which offers a very large variety of articles for sale, including books, the section entitled 'Sex in Marriage?' contains the following:

When marriage grows cold, it is often because the demands of her home and her married life have made a wife forget that the intimate side of her life is just as important as a well-cared-for home. But it is: as much so as the cosy corner in the living-room, and the Sunday joint.

The 'cosy corner in the living-room' inserted as a status symbol, indicates that this kind of manipulation is directed at the lower middle class downwards, and not, as previous studies might have led one to suppose, at the middle class proper.

But it would be wrong to see the pressures of advertising, which keeps people in a constant state of unfulfillable fore-pleasure, as the only force militating against contentment in modern marriage. More important are the effects of work. These can sometimes be so damaging that sexuality cannot even survive as a special treat for high days and holidays, its traditional place in industrial societies. Rainwater's statistics (pp. 56–7 above) show that a significant number of people with the most alienating kind of work became virtually sexless in their married life. With the continuing sexualization of other sectors of experience, this is bound to bring about a contradiction within the institution of marriage, which could produce socially undesirable consequences for the state of married life. All married people, however much they may have allowed themselves to be manipulated, inevitably become aware of these difficulties, and now a specific branch of manipulation has been developed to cope with it. The problems are 'openly discussed' and always declared to be susceptible to individual resolution. In a West German inquiry in the sixties more people declared themselves personally 'satisfied' with their marriage than they did in the fifties. This 'satisfaction' is reflected by the stable divorce rate of the last few years. The stabilization which has occurred is of course not necessarily identical with sexual satisfaction, or even with the ideological concept of the 'happy marriage'; it seems very much on the evidence as if it were the result of mounting social controls, which have engendered the inability to see that if one feels unhappy, then, objectively, one *is* unhappy. The catalogue quoted above reads like a black Utopia, with its descriptions of articles for restoring the faculty for enjoyment taken away by work, and further, to prevent the victims from even seeing that their unhappiness is real. An aphrodisiac 'Cythera Cocktail' is described as follows:

If everything still seems too workaday, if you can't quite enter into the harmonious romantic mood in which to enjoy each other's company to the full, then you should try drinking a glass of Cythera. Cythera Cocktail sweeps away that everyday feeling, and makes both of you equally inclined for love.

All this seems to be the very opposite of promiscuity. And so it is. Even the continually rising rate of extra-marital intercourse in the last fifty years cannot yet be taken as a tendency to promiscuity, for this still only applies to 'bourgeois' circles, in the USA just as much as in Germany, as Kinsey's findings show. Indeed the term *promiscuity* presupposes not only frequency of extra-marital intercourse, but also a specific kind of object-choice, namely a partial or total indifference in the choice. This form of sexual behaviour is certainly not connected to the institution of marriage. But just as certainly, it occurs historically as a reaction to monogamous marriage, and is today particularly prevalent among married people.

One of the most modern ways of adapting sexually to marriage being propagated at present is to indulge in extra-marital affairs with the blessing of one's marriage partner, or at least, not with any open protest on his or her part.

The only material we have on this is a report on 'group sex in the USA', the so-called Leigh Report, originally published in America as *The Velvet Underground*, which, apart from its confused style, gives no statistics. It does, however, offer a vast amount of material which can be broken down into the following conclusions.

The sexual behaviour described occurred predominantly in married circles. The people concerned had sexual intercourse with as many and as different people as they could, regardless of their sex or whether they were married or not. The couples generally indulged in these activities as a pair, seldom separately.

This behaviour is spread over the whole of North America and Canada; it is not known in what exact numbers, or in what portion to the population. Leigh alone was able to get in touch with over five hundred married men in the course of six months who were willing to offer him their wives, with the latters' consent. Before this he had no experience at all in how to make this kind of contact. A fairly small number of single men and women were willing to make a similar arrangement with him.

This kind of behaviour is practised in particular by people in the higher professional group, but not by those who happen to be very mobile for work or other reasons. Groups among which it is particularly prevalent are architects, nurses, engineers, shop owners and civil servants.

The promiscuous individuals, especially the married couples, are on average unusually well adjusted and conformist socially. They do not have any fewer children than monogamous married couples. 'In all other cases the husbands had profitable private businesses or well-paid jobs, and only sold obscene photographs of themselves and their wives as a hobby on the side.'[1] 'The couple from Oregon had had no pre-marital experience; they had loved each other in high school, and marriage came as the

[1] All quotations are translated from the German edition.

crowning experience to their romance.' . . . 'They saw a small ad. in a magazine which awakened their curiosity, and suddenly found themselves in the sex market. They are in their late thirties, and have two pre-teenage boys. The husband is an independent contractor. They are regular church-goers.' . . . 'There is nothing about the subject they do not know, and yet they want to hear it all over and over again. They want to have proof that they are not alone, that they are normal!' Leigh claims that these couples bring up their children 'exceptionally well' but he has only their word for it.

Those concerned have only grasped certain fragments of an anti-puritan ideology, if at all. Their critique of prevailing conditions never transcends the characteristically puritan, anti-human and two-faced sexual morality of American society. Many of them practise sado-masochistic techniques. Some claim that this is only a hobby – though it has become a necessary one – and that they are not driven to it by any kind of basic compulsion. A special industry has grown up to meet the needs of these variations, though, it should be added, it was not specifically this kind of 'family' promiscuity which originally brought it forth. There is a special catalogue for this type of sadism, with the title 'For all lovers of binding and domestic chastisement'. In the section entitled 'Leather' alone, the following articles were offered for sale: 'Clubs with leather leashes, manacles for knees, ankles and wrists, leather helmets, leather gloves, leather gas masks, leather arm-protectors, leather neck bands, leather cuffs, leather machine-guns, whips with leather lashes, chastity belts, leather skirts, leather masks.' The prices for each article are between ten and forty dollars.

Everything is photographed. The preservation of sexual activities on film and the exchange, study, posting to other people and systematic collection of home-photographed nude pornography seems to be an indispensable part of family promiscuity. One sometimes has the impression that this kind of photography has taken over direct from the family album; certainly photography and showing photographs round is as compulsory a part of this kind of hobby as it is of traditional family outings. One couple refused a special request that came to them by post 'because they could now scarcely imagine sensual pleasures without spectators and the clicking of cameras'. 'The couples who practise so-called "domestic chastisement" are not content with only exchanging photographs with other married couples, but have the peculiar need to keep on drawing more and more people into their circle.' A husband writes in an advertisement: 'We like almost anything, but especially anything unusual. We have a polaroid camera, which has already given us a great deal of fun at parties.' This compulsive photographing and collection of photos is not simply a form of voyeurism and exhibitionism run wild.

Very often these individuals 'draw the line at one thing'. This 'one thing' varies greatly; it is often homosexuality, even more often passive anal intercourse, occasionally special idiosyncrasies. For example: 'This couple had an aversion to hair. They had evolved a special method of removing hair, which guaranteed that there would be no "scratchy aftergrowth". . . . They had a large circle of acquaintances, including some who could not comply with their requirements. They had no children, and complained that the chattering of the other couple's children had spoilt their fun: "We spent the night with another couple where there were three kids sleeping in the next room; we found that put us off a lot." '

The people concerned generally claim that love and sex are quite different things, that they love each other, and that in order to love each other properly, they need the widest possible sexual variety and experience. 'This woman was constantly in search of new pleasures, always with the consent of her husband. She had tried anal intercourse, but found it too uncomfortable to be satisfying; however, she was so eager to "try everything" that she had agreed with her husband that the Canadian should show her next time, since he was not quite so well endowed. . . . She had a passion for animals. . . . She said among other things . . . "We enjoyed it so much, and I mean we . . . he enjoyed it just as much as I did. . . . It's so exciting!" ' According to another woman 'everyone agreed that they had got a much more real, complex and honest attitude to sex than most other married couples'. They thought a lot of them had avoided divorce in this way, and were convinced they had a happy married and family life. They claimed not to suffer from any of the frustration or 'periods of coldness' which caused trouble in other marriages, or the kind of resentment which often attacks one partner, and nearly drives the other to despair. Further it was claimed that not one of the group 'stepped outside it'.

Leigh sees the special danger of this kind of behaviour to lie in 'its tendency to spread like an epidemic'. 'If one can get used to one particular sexual partner, then one can get used to any sexual partner.' This would undermine the basis of western civilization. He sees the strict enforcement of legal sanctions as the best way of fighting the menace, especially control of the post. Leigh's view is not a particularly relevant one. His 'epidemic' theory is quite certainly superficial; all it claims is that there is a social law underlying this type of behaviour. But can it be accepted that there is a special law underlying the spread of 'non-selective' sex? The problem is a difficult one to resolve, because the existing material, even in the field of sexual criminology,[2] does not permit any definite conclusions. Traditional sexual pathology certainly does not account for behaviour of this type. For according to its model – which is also Freud's – every society has its quota of abnormal individuals, who are possessed by one instinct or another to a degree far exceeding the usual social measure of irregularity. These people provide the counterbalancing influence in the formation of a norm. In any society, they give rise to a constant degree of crime, perversion, psychosis, etc.

In critical discussion and non-dogmatic socialist literature promiscuity is often put forward as the form of sexuality most suited to socialist practice. It is regarded as a blow against the repressive implications of 'falling in love', love itself, and bourgeois marriage, and in favour of the abolition of private property. And it is true that being in love, as well as loving, like all known historical and current forms of marriage and family life implies ownership to some degree. The question is, however, whether this kind of ownership is always bad, in that it must of necessity create a repressive context of private property, with all the harmful effects on the individual and social character that this implies, or whether, in circumstances where the love-object is autonomously and consciously chosen, it can be conceivable and legitimate. It seems unlikely that even the most muddled and unreflecting advocates of the abolition of the repressive triangle, love-sexuality-ownership, would have proposed *this* method of overcoming the repressive organization of sexuality. The promiscuity recommended by well-meaning but short-sighted socialists is itself highly repressive, and bound to stabilize authoritarian and antiquated forms of social organization. The cases described by Leigh chiefly demonstrate that the individuals in question work off the discontentment that they feel with their lives by indulging in what is virtually a sport. Even when they get addicted, as is nearly always the case, they do not see it as a sign that their way of life is not fulfilling their needs, but as an increased attachment to their sport. The reigning form of sexual

---

[2] The material quoted and analysed in *Sex Offenders* does not provide any relevant information either.

relationship, the *compulsorily* monogamous and permanent partnership, or, better still, the compulsory *use* of a single partner, is not genuinely superseded when people compulsorily abolish all rules and all selectiveness from their sex lives. For this 'lack of rules' has rules of its own, and makes differences of its own, which are pathologically bound to the constraints of the ruling monogamous arrangement.

These individuals are in fact highly adjusted to their society. They have found the diversity necessary to reconcile them with their workaday world, and they live for 'fun'. They are acting on a need to repeat an injury done to them at a pre-Oedipal stage. They seem to be saying: if I can't be happy with one beloved person, then love is not worth anything, and I will at least have my revenge on the person who refused me by having sex with everyone and everything. These people too put up an extraordinarily convincing genital façade, only to hide their pre-genital wounds. Sexuality becomes radically similar to the capitalist form of consumption, in which goods have no intrinsic worth outside the value attributed to them by advertising and the rising scale on which they are consumed. Translated into sexual terms, the principle is: I get no satisfaction from any individual thing I buy because I can only wear it out, not really use it. Therefore I might as well wear it out thoroughly, give it the highest possible market value and persuade other people of its merits, photograph it, collect it, treat it sadistically, etc. That this is a form of fetishism, and bears a strong resemblance to current attitudes to consumer goods, will be made clear by this example from the Leigh report, which is far from being an exceptional case:

There were sixteen photographs in all. Two showed the couple in bathing trunks and bikini, the others showed them in every conceivable sexual combination, including coitus, fellatio, cunnilingus and lesbian acts; for these a second girl had been brought in. This pictorial material was intended to show potential participants the sensual delights awaiting them. Some of the photos showed the man and woman naked and looking as suggestive as possible, with the female charms fully displayed, and in one case showing the man with penis in erection. There were also half-nudes, with the woman in a bra and fur panties – ostensibly mink – and another of her naked except for her shoes and a fur coat. . . . There was a photo which showed the wife in coitus with the husband, sitting astride him in riding position, while the Swedish girl knelt smiling in front of them – slightly sideways in order not to block her friend the photographer's view – giving the couple manual assistance.

There was another photo of the trio in similar pose but with the girl in the position previously occupied by the wife, while the latter helped them manually, also smiling. ... What was not to be seen in the photographs was described in writing. The intention of all this was to bring together as many married and unmarried 'converts' as possible.

The classic exhibitionist's behaviour implies the unspoken demand: 'Look! I'm not castrated, even though I'm afraid of it', or 'Castrate me!' and, simultaneously, 'Look, I'm so strong that I can even show you my penis.' This train of thought is similar to that of the fetishist who protects himself from the fear of castration by projecting a penis onto the woman. The married couples in this report seem to be equally hag-ridden by the fear of not being fully genital in their sexual selves. But their attempts to overcome the fear of castration remain at a pre-genital stage: they 'show off' their phallic capacity. Like the exhibitionist, they continuously have to prove that they 'really are' fully genital. But they go a step further. Their collections of photos are intended to say to the outside world 'We suffer under the genital demands of marriage and love – look, we are busy throwing all the mud we can at them. But don't dare touch our genital façade of love and marriage – look at the fun and excitement we get from it!'

This background throws light on why several of the couples felt impelled to remove their body hair, and why several felt repulsed by the proximity of children (one couple did both). The removal of hair is a castration act for both men and women (shaving off, removing), and also an attempt to regain a childhood (pre-genital) state in which the skin was still smooth. The distaste for children ('squeaking rats', whose presence disturbs coitus) is a manifest attempt to ward off the unconscious and forbidden wish to live out one's desire in a childish manner ('squeaking with pleasure').

There are three main factors which oppose the development of a genital character, i.e. one capable of full genital sexual enjoyment, and one equipped with all the non-sexual attributes that normally go with such a state:
— Insufficient preparation for genital organization by the family and the outside world. Faulty educational techniques and adverse social influences render the child incapable, or partially incapable of transforming the early biologically determined stages of sexual development (oral, anal and phallic) in such a way that they can later be united into a genital whole.
— Alienating work which has adverse effects on sexual practice. Not only the performance principle in itself but the meaningless nature of the performance required, blocks and damages the

individual's capacity for feeling. He finds himself helplessly repeating the repressive circumstances of work and the consumer society in his sex life.

— The overwhelming genital demands of society. Insufficiently developed and integrated individuals are put under pressure by advertising, the consumer system, and various forms of social and sexual compulsion to conform, to behave as though their sexual selves really were fully genital.

It is the last factor above all which forces the individual to put up a genital façade, and the less genital he really is, the more ostentatious it has to be. The form of promiscuity described above is but *one* way of keeping up such a genital façade. There are pathological alternatives: for example, conforming rigidly to a role, such as marrying early before personal or social maturity has been reached, or else not keeping up the façade at all and becoming perverted or schizophrenic. For an illustration of the former reaction, see p. 93, note 28; the latter reaction is to be found in numerous case histories of schizophrenia. Promiscuity is most readily available as an alternative to people in the 'free' professions, since they are the people with the most opportunity for escaping the pressures and norms of their professional and social roles in *one way* (sexuality) without the world around them noticing and exacting penalties. Even if the type of promiscuity which we have described does not occur on a statistically large scale, it is still a sign that broad groups of the population are breaking down under the pressure of socio-sexual demands with which they are not equipped to cope.

### DATING AS PREPARATION FOR MARRIAGE

'Apart from the natural physical vigour, the two chief characteristics of American youth are the relative lack of responsibility, and dating', wrote Geoffrey Gorer in his anthropological study *The Americans*.[3] Dating in the USA is the 'normal' form of sexual behaviour between the beginning of puberty and marriage, It has the 'official' role of preparing for marriage, and 'centring' the young person on heterosexual relationships after puberty. This kind of sexual practice, in such a highly normative and institutionalized form, is unique to the USA among industrialized countries. The following are its main features.

Almost everybody from all social classes begins to participate in it at the onset of puberty.

[3] Geoffrey Gorer: *The Americans – a study in national character*, London, 1948, p. 93.

There are a number of rules – differing from class to class and area to area, but always strict – to which the participants have to conform. Their prestige inside and outside the peer group depends on the extent and degree to which they fulfil the demands of these rules. In order not to be excluded from the dating system altogether, they have to be able to demonstrate a definite minimum of success in fulfilment of the rules (for example a certain number of dates within a certain time). Pertaining to these rules there are hard and fast formulae of conduct: how one introduces oneself to potential dates, and what one does together at what stage (invitation out to a meal, then a dance, kissing, exchange of caresses of a mounting degree of intimacy).

The prestige for boys lies in taking out as many girls as possible in a certain space of time, and getting as quickly as possible to the stage of exchanged caresses; for girls it lies in the length of time they can make the boy wait for these caresses. Both sexes are reckoned successful if they seem very self-confident. In addition they have to fulfil a number of very 'difficult' rules which look to the outsider very like the requirements of a primitive totemistic cult. Gorer writes:

Participation in the dating pattern is somewhat different for the two sexes: all boys can and should take part in it, the level to which they aspire being dependent on their qualifications; but only the most successful and popular girls do so fully, the rest having to be content with a steady boy friend, or even the companionship of a fellow unfortunate. . . . For many girls consequently, the dating period is one of humiliation, of frustration, of failure. But, though it is painful, it is not usually psychologically crippling.[4]

Dating claims to be a game, an 'as if' form of sexuality. The participants may well see it with the same eyes as naïve parents do children's playing-at-doctors. 'Dating is idiosyncratic in many ways, but especially so in that it uses the language and gestures of courtship and love-making without implying the reality of either.'[5] But this 'as if' form is regulated by more stringent norms than the social and sexual behaviour of any known primitive or civilized culture:

A number of societies, of which the Samoans and the Trobrianders are well-known examples, allow for a period of sexual licence and experiment before betrothal and marriage; but these are, and are meant to be, years of sensual and sexual satisfaction, sought for their own sake. In American dating sensual and sexual satisfaction may play a part

[4] op. cit., pp. 84–5.    [5] op. cit., p. 81.

(though this is by no means necessary) as counters in the game, but they are not the object of the exercise. . . . [6]

The real object of the exercise is the gratification of narcissism. Dating belongs most firmly in the category of narcissistic object-choice (to be loved, not to love). Love is in fact the most complete expression of defeat, and puts an end to the 'game'. So dating cannot be seen as a preparatory to petting, petting being defined as love-play with everything but genital union. This can naturally be a part of dating, but it has only the same generalized value in the 'points system' as for example sending or receiving presents of flowers.

'Dating is a highly patterned activity or group of activities, comparable in some ways to a formal dance, in others to a very complicated competitive game.' The 'competitive game' ends with the victory of one partner or with a draw. A draw entails both partners leaving the game feeling 'their self-esteem, their assurance, enhanced'.[7] 'The victor is the one who makes the other lose self-control without losing it him- (or her-) self.'[8] An example of this would be a girl making a boy have an orgasm without 'losing her head' or a boy managing to get a girl to have intercourse with him. J. R. Udry in his comprehensive book on marriage calls dating a 'zero-sum game'. But he claims that the defeated partner is only despised in lower-class or cross-class dating circumstances.

Generally sexual intercourse means the breakdown of the game in middle-class dating, because it shows that the girl has taken the situation seriously. In lower-class and cross-class dating it implies to the boy that the girl has lost, because these groups think of dating as a 'zero-sum game' in which the purpose, for the man, is to conquer.[9]

What Udry says about the lower class is true, and has been confirmed by other studies.[10] But a large number of analyses and findings on dating behaviour among young people at college have shown that Udry was wrong to confine it to the lower class. Young people in the lower class are simply more direct in their sexual behaviour (as in their speech and gestures), and so are more likely to make no bones about publicizing their victory.

[6] op. cit., p. 82.

[7] op. cit., pp. 81–2.

[8] op. cit., p. 88.

[9] J. Richard Udry: *The Social Context of Marriage*, Philadelphia and New York, 1966, p. 114.

[10] For example Rainwater in 'Some Aspects of Lower Class Sexual Behaviour', quoted above (p. 55).

There are three important socio/psychological factors connected with the dating system. Firstly, it is especially suited to the production of the most minute status differences within a professional group or social stratum. Secondly, sexuality as a whole is demeaned by dating. To discuss the whole of the specific way in which this is brought about would lead us into repeating points already covered; we shall consequently only be dealing with one question, that of empathy in the dating situation. Thirdly, there is a special connexion between dating and the incidence of latent homosexuality in the USA. In the rest of this section we will deal briefly with all these factors.

In order to be accounted sexually attractive, a young person has to fulfil a large number of social criteria which have nothing to do with his or her sexuality or character If these conditions are not fulfilled the person will, like the lower-class girl in Udry's account of cross-class dating, be despised by the person from the class above. This behaviour creates and perpetuates extremely depersonalized and authoritarian qualities and performance norms in the people concerned. The nature of the primary control is very clearly demonstrated by the statistics obtained by Rogers and Havens in their analysis of dating.[11] The statistics refer to 'fraternities' and 'sororities'. These are student clubs, for men and women respectively, and their prestige relates closely to the parents' social status. In a large number of them the members must be able to show a certain weekly minimum of dates. Since in most American colleges the students all

Table 4

Dating relationships of fraternity students to girl students and non-students

|  | Fraternity with high prestige | Fraternity with moderate prestige | Fraternity with low prestige |
|---|---|---|---|
| Sorority with high prestige | 29 | 16 | 6 |
| Sorority with moderate prestige | 20 | 12 | 7 |
| Sorority with low prestige | 14 | 24 | 10 |
| Girls' dormitory | 14 | 25 | 25 |
| Girls not studying at this college | 24 | 43 | 52 |
| total | 100% | 100% | 100% |

[11] E. M. Rogers and Eugene Havens: 'Prestige Rating and Male Selection on a College Campus' in *Marriage and Family Living*, no. 22, February 1960.

live on the campus, 'dormitory' means a general students' hostel, inhabited by the students with the lowest social prestige (who were not accepted by the sorority and fraternity house on the campus) or by 'outsiders' who did not want to join a club.

Let us now turn to the reduction of sexuality which is caused and maintained by the institutionalized system for learning sexual relations that is embodied in dating. In the study from which Table 4 is taken, 'Empathy as a Process in the Dating Situation?'[12], Stewart and Vernon come to the not surprising conclusion that two people gain more empathy for each other, the more they go out together. The really surprising discovery they made was that the capacity for empathy does not increase with relative frequency of dates. People with a large number of dates stay at the same emotional distance from their boy-friends or girl-friends as people with very few dates. To us this would seem to indicate – though this is not the conclusion drawn by the authors of the study – that individuals emerge from the dating process as helpless and psychologically undeveloped as they went in, and that they only develop the capacity for empathy when they start going steady or become engaged. But the damage has been done: this capacity has to build on the imperfect foundations laid by the individual's dating experience, and so remains permanently handicapped.[13] One very small part of this 'damage' comes to light in an empirical study by Kirkpatrick and Kanin of 'Male Sex Aggression on a University Campus'.[14] Fifty-six per cent of the girls questioned in this study claimed to have been 'offended' at least once in that particular scholastic year! These 163 offended girls had been subjected to a total of 1,022 'offensive episodes', that is to say, sexual behaviour from dating partners which they themselves believed they did not want. Table 5 shows: (i) how these girls reacted emotionally to the behaviour in question, and (ii) how they behaved, in relation to the boy and their immediate society.

Further light is shed on these statistics when one remembers that at least the second two categories of sexual 'offence' (petting

[12] R. L. Stewart and G. M. Vernon: 'Empathy as a Process in the Dating Situation?' in *American Sociological Review*, vol. XXII, no. 1, 1957, pp. 48–52.
[13] The psychological and social consequences of dating cannot be compared to those of petting in a direct sense. Petting can be a perfectly adequate form of preparation for genital intercourse – though with a few specific reservations (for example, the increased danger of later only being able to achieve orgasm through oral or manual stimulation, if petting has been the only form of sexual satisfaction for 'too long' – see Kinsey).
[14] C. Kirkpatrick and E. Kanin: 'Male Sex Aggression on a University Campus' in *American Sociological Review*, vol. XXII, no. 1, 1957, pp. 52–8.

below the waist, and attempted intercourse) represent later stages of dating behaviour, i.e. when young people have been out together a number of times, and could be imagined to have got to know each other 'more closely'.

Table 5

1. Emotional reactions of offended respondents by level of erotic intimacy:

| Girls' emotional reactions | Necking and petting above the waist | Petting below the waist | Attempted intercourse and attempted intercourse with violence |
|---|---|---|---|
| Anger | 48 | 42 | 35 |
| Guilt | 19 | 26 | 21 |
| Fear | 14 | 23 | 38 |
| Disgust, disillusionment or confusion | 18 | 9 | 6 |

2. Answers of respondents to the question 'What did you do?'

| | | | |
|---|---|---|---|
| Selective avoidance | 37 | 25 | 31 |
| Discussion and warning re age group | 34 | 20 | 16 |
| Secrecy | 19 | 46 | 49 |
| Discussion with aggressor | 3 | 4 | 4 |
| Report to authority | 7 | 5 | — |
| total | 100% | 100% | 100% |

However imprecise and superficial the categories underlying this study may be, it does make one thing very clear: that a large number of girls who take part in this form of institutionalized sexual behaviour have alarming experiences. Only a very small minority is capable of discussing it with the boy concerned, and in any case the frequent change of partner which is built into the institution makes this an impossibility. These results are all the more significant in that the girls questioned did after all belong to the best educated section of the population, the one therefore which could be expected to be best able to communicate their experiences and their distress. Gorer's conclusion that people who have derived their previous sexual experience from dating move from it to marriage without being 'psychologically crippled' is certainly extremely naïve; at the very least it would seem to imply a highly superficial conception of mental health.

In our enumeration of dating's chief characteristics, we did not mention its most advanced form: *double-dating*. This means that two 'buddies', among college students very often room-mates, take out a girl or two girls together. These two friends always have closer emotional ties to each other than to the girl or girls. Their friendship outlasts the dating sequence; indeed the latter may have the hidden purpose of strengthening the former. This kind of relationship might be interpreted as a cultural move to channel the unstable sexual urges of puberty, which still hover between both sexes, onto a heterosexual course. Youthful friendships in bourgeois culture certainly do fulfil that role. But this view is somewhat undermined by the fact that double-dating goes on until the end of the individual's dating period, and often comes to an unmediated end when one of the parties suddenly gets engaged or married. In this context marriage looks like an artificial stabilization of the sexual character into a genital mode which in reality has not been attained. This sup-position is strengthened by the fact that the dating system is compulsively heterosexual, and also semi-promiscuous, which allows the participants to set up a genital façade while remain-ing infantile in their object-choice. While still continuing to believe that the system does no harm to mental health, Gorer himself cites two factors in confirmation of the supposition above, referring to the United States army in which young men have to serve immediately after the dating period. This differs from all other armies firstly in that all men suspected of homo-sexuality are excluded from it (this is one of the specific points in the selection of conscripts). Secondly, the authorities deliber-ately attempt to keep the heterosexual interests of the soldiers alive, to such a degree that the army tends to strike a foreigner as being in 'a state of exacerbated erethism'.[15]

This 'exacerbated erethism' reminds one of the 'ostentatious sexuality' of the promiscuous married couples, who have like-wise not achieved fully developed heterosexuality. One is further strengthened in this conclusion when one hears that Americans do not so much experience the dislike, disgust and repulsion in the face of homosexuality, which prevents bour-geois individuals from giving open expression to any tendencies they themselves may have in that direction, as rather a panic fear of it. 'It is seen as an immediate and personal threat . . . a drastic threat to a man's integrity and is reacted to with violence and panic.'[16] The tendency to early marriage in the USA, perhaps

[15] Gorer: op. cit., p. 97.    [16] op. cit., p. 95.

also in other late capitalist countries,[17] and especially the tendency among the American middle classes to marry 'suddenly', as soon as the external framework of 'play' promiscuity provided by college life is withdrawn, is more indicative of a need to prop up the sexual and character structure, than of an integrated genital character.

## LATENT HOMOSEXUALITY AND THE 'CONVERGENCE' OF THE SEXES

Psycho-analysis differentiates between manifest and latent homosexuality. The former is characterized by object-choice centring exclusively or mainly on persons of the individual's own sex. The term 'latent homosexuality' expresses the fact that, 'in addition to their manifest heterosexuality, a very considerable measure of latent or unconscious homosexuality can be detected in all normal people'.[18] According to this conception, 'all human beings are capable of making a homosexual object-choice and have in fact made one in their unconscious. Indeed, libidinal attachments to persons of the same sex play no less a part as factors in normal mental life, and a greater part as a motive force for illness, than do similar attachments to the opposite sex.'[19] This means that the sex drive is initially independent of the objects on which it later fixes itself. The static category corresponding to this dynamic conception of homosexuality is the 'constitutional bisexuality' of human beings: homosexuality and heterosexuality are *learned*, as cultural achievements. In addition to the cultural achievement discussed above, and the individual achievement which sometimes has to follow of gathering in all the component instincts under the primacy of the genital, a person also has to learn the faculty for heterosexual object-choice. More accurately, both begin to occur as historically recognizable entities at the same time, and mutually control and complete each other.

[17] At this point it could be objected that this tendency to early marriage has also been noted in the socialist countries, and so must depend on a factor beyond the specific way in which the forces of production are organized, something in the fact of industrialization itself. However, closer examination of the highly industrialized capitalist and socialist countries would certainly reveal that the tendency to early marriage in the socialist countries depends upon other factors than in the capitalist countries. Current examples of such a factor would be the *direct* suppression of pre-marital sexual strivings there, and also the 'socialist' morality of family life, propaganda for it, etc.

[18] Freud: *The Psychogenesis of a Case of Homosexuality in a Woman*, 1920, op. cit., vol. XVIII, p. 171

[19] Freud: *Three Essays on Sexuality*, p. 145.

This conception does not exclude the possibility that the final choice between homosexuality and heterosexuality cannot be partially, or even totally 'decided for' the individual by some factor in his or her constitutional make-up. Freud ascribed great importance to this possibility in all his clinical discussions on homosexuality. But this does not mean that the constitutional factor in homosexuality (about which, incidentally, science has discovered little more than was known in Freud's day) is the same as 'innate homosexuality'. This exists just as much, and just as little, as innate heterosexuality. The anal elements in homosexual attitudes cannot, any more than any other fixation, be said to be basic to homosexuality. These components indicate a fixation at a certain stage of sexual development which have nothing to do with homosexuality, and produce a certain personality-type which, again, need not be homosexual.[20] Fully developed genital homosexuality is capable, like heterosexuality, of dependent and narcissistic object-choice, though it often seems to be characterized by an 'inclination towards a narcissistic object-choice'.[21]

Culturally, homosexuality means that a person has got to a certain point along the route from the original bisexual state to the socially acceptable state of genital heterosexuality, and stayed there. At the same time it is very difficult to distinguish between the 'genital' moment and the 'heterosexual' moment, and quite impossible if one follows Freud's definition of what constitutes the normal, healthy, realistic individual. In present circumstances, homosexuality is inevitably accompanied by certain specific kinds of damage to the instinct structure. But these kinds of damage are not only relative to the social and personal demands of the ruling reality principle, they are above all a result of the psychological compulsions by means of which the reality principle enforces its norms in the process of socialization. All mechanisms and blockages held to be responsible for homosexuality – symbiotic attachment to the mother, infantile narcissism, fear of castration, flight from masculine rivalry – are not exclusive to homosexuality:[22] they can equally well produce a neurotic heterosexual personality. Even if the incidence of

---

[20] See Freud: *Three Essays on Sexuality*, p. 152: 'The playing of a sexual part by the mucous membrane of the anus is by no means limited to intercourse between men: preference for it is in no way characteristic of inverted feeling.'

[21] Freud: *Some Neurotic Mechanisms in Jealousy, Paranoia and Homosexuality*, 1922, op. cit., vol. XVIII, p. 230.

[22] See Freud: op. cit., p. 231.

neurosis in the broadest sense (that is, including all 'non-clinical cases' as well) is higher among homosexuals than heterosexuals, the fault for this would lie, above all, in the social taboo which weighs so heavily on homosexuality. All homosexuals suffer under this taboo in one way or another, through either tacit or open persecution and punishment. It can therefore work as a factor in the 'unleashing of neurosis' in a way that heterosexuality cannot.[23]

All this is not a justification of homosexuality as a type of object-choice. It would only be possible to do justice to homosexuality in the context of a really free community, in which all the individual kinds of damage at present suffered by homosexuals and heterosexuals alike had become superfluous. In such a society, compulsive homosexual fixation would also become superfluous. Only then could it be determined, on the basis of empirical research and analysis, whether homosexuality still occurred, quasi-naturally, even when the component instincts were organized in a completely non-repressive way into genital primacy, and if people had a perfect psychological and social freedom in their choice of love-object. It could then also be discovered whether a non-regressive, non-infantile bisexuality were also possible. It could be that homosexuality would 'die out' in a free society; that we cannot know at the moment. For the time being all pronouncements about a 'natural preponderance of heterosexuality in the pleasure-organization of the individual' or 'constitutional homosexual factors' are really only speculation. In a free society they would be a matter of experience, and such tendencies could be integrated non-compulsively into the socializing process in children and young people.

Because manifest homosexuality is subject to such a strong social taboo – which far exceeds the stringency of the law in this matter – even latent homosexual urges ('libidinal attachments to persons of the same sex') can only play a very ambivalent role in the formation of libidinal relationships as a whole. The socially dominant form of latent homosexuality is repressed homosexuality.

[23] See Adorno: 'Sexualtabus und Recht Heute' ('Sexual Taboos and the Law Today') in *Eingriffe*, Frankfurt, 1963, p. 112: 'If my observation is correct, it is particularly noticeable among intellectually gifted homosexuals that their productivity is psychologically hampered; they are not able to achieve their potential. One of the reasons for this is the permanent pressure they are under from anxiety, and from society's attitude to them. Public opinion inspired the laws against them, and these laws in turn reinforced the negative character of public opinion.'

The tension set up by the opposition of unconscious willing-
ness and conscious unwillingness (horror, disgust, fear, lack of
interest), reinforced by social taboo, brings about a vast collective repression. As such it can serve as the socio-psychological
basis for highly aggressive, individual and collective destructive
behaviour, and for corresponding political movements.

It was a historical mutation of latent homosexuality which
played an important role in the growth and cohesion of the
fascist mass movement in Germany. Erich Fromm, writing in
1936, analysed this historical mutation in *Autorität und Familie*,
giving it the name of 'the authoritarian-masochistic character':

Here we ought to mention the fact that sado-masochism generally
goes with a relatively low degree of genital heterosexuality. This has
two consequences. Firstly, that pre-genital and particularly anal
instincts are relatively strongly developed and find expression in
character traits such as orderliness, punctuality and thrift, which play
such an evident and socially important role in the character of the
petty-bourgeois authoritarian type. The other consequence is the
presence of homosexual instincts. The extent to which the sado-
masochistic instinct structure is connected with homosexuality is as
yet a largely unsolved problem.... The love-life of this type of person
is curiously divided. Physiologically, the average authoritarian man is
heterosexual. In his emotions, however, he is homosexual. In other
words, in his physical relationship to woman, in terms of satisfying
bodily needs, he is potent, and heterosexual in behaviour in so far as
he is capable of begetting children and founding a family. But in terms
of emotion he is homosexual, and is hostile and cruel to woman. This
homosexual streak quite often turns into homosexuality in the precise
sense, as can be seen in the extremist authoritarian structures of recent
times. The cases of manifest homosexuality are not however the most
sociologically important. More important is the tender and loving
masochistic relationship developed by a weaker man towards a strong
one. This is a very important factor in the structure we are discussing,
and becomes more so, the more irrational the relationship is in terms
of the social situation, and the more it goes against the real interests of
the weaker person.[24]

In contrast to this, the most recent epoch of capitalist rule has
produced a change in the role of latent homosexuality. Contemporary forms of socialization, particularly advertising and the
direction of consumption, but even the repressive organization

[24] Erich Fromm: *Autorität und Familie*, vol. 5 of *Schriften des Instituts für
Sozialforschung* (Papers of the Institute for Social Research), ed. Max Horkheimer, Paris, 1936, pp. 125ff.

of the family, show a diminishing stress on the development of the anal qualities. The component instincts are now being manipulated as a whole, allowed a certain degree of liberty and then rendered socially 'harmless' by the compulsion to genital behaviour. This further weakens genital sexuality, but it does mean that heterosexuality loses some of its externally more threatening aspects which used to cause the sado-masochistic personality type to react so anxiously and aggressively to woman. Adorno makes a meaningful comment, which he does not however follow up, about this contemporary development, to the effect that 'in the twentieth century, possibly because of an unconscious homosexualizing of society, the erotic ideal is becoming infantile, and we now set on a pedestal what thirty or forty years ago was referred to with lascivious alarm as a "child woman".'[25]

'Homosexualizing' is however too neutral a term. Homosexuality is quite frequently a source of exquisite phallic and genital experience, and one which it quite in accordance with an ego-syntonic character structure, that is to say one in which the ego is perfectly well integrated. But at present latent homosexual drives are forcibly pressed into the service of the genital façade. The authoritarian/masochistic character, conscious of his own genital weakness, felt he was not adequate to cope with the opposite sex. Today, both sexes are adopting all kinds of almost manifestly 'homosexual' attributes, in behaviour, appearance, clothing, speech and gesture. Men wear long hair and walk erotically, girls in the autumn of 1967 were wearing aggressive, 'masculine' fashion accessories of all kinds, such as thick chains round the waist with trousers and skirts, knee-high boots resembling riding boots, panama hats tied under the chin; both sexes buy their clothes in the fashionable men's boutiques. But this is simply the 'homosexualized' surface of what is basically an infantile structure. Underneath a 'levelling out of tension between the sexes' is taking place. People are regressing collectively to an infantile stage. Viewed critically as an ideological and historical phenomenon, this represents the breaking up of the bourgeois type of genital sexuality with its specifically masculine and feminine characteristics. Peter Furth gives this explanation, in a discussion with Herbert Marcuse:

Society is founded on contradictions and so it is in its own interest to lessen the tension between them as much as it possibly can. One of the ways it does this is to weaken the tension between the sexes, and filter it off into new roles which entail less tension. This makes possible the

[25] 'Sexualtabus und Recht heute', op. cit., p. 113.

thing we were talking about before, indirect repression without the use of taboos. Taboos cause opposition, and opposition must not become conscious. The thing has to be done by sleight of hand, it has to be censored, so to speak, before it can be noticed and reacted against. This kind of repression is much more subtle and secret and consequently much more effective.[26]

The paradigm of a tensionless state is the child's temporary complete gratification after it has been fed. The psychological phenomenon corresponding to the historical one is a desire to cease to belong to one sex or the other. It was this central aspect that Adorno meant when he said that 'the erotic ideal is becoming infantile'. But – and this refers back to previous observations – though differentiations may have dissolved at the level of psychic structure, people still have an 'artificial' social and genital adulthood 'superimposed' over the infantile self beneath. The result is the continuance of male dominance (which has economically been superseded) as well as its attendant taboos (prohibition of homosexuality).

At the same time, there is one highly advantageous, almost utopian aspect to this breakdown of differentiation between the sexes. Individual taste at last has free play, and people have the opportunity to develop internal qualities and relations with others according to personal inclination. Peter Brückner, talking about the First Commune in Berlin, noted as a progressive aspect that 'it had made people aware of their faculty for making very minute cognitive distinctions'. The highly developed ego was able to express its own degree of originality through the minute distinctions it was able to make in its observation of the world. Tension between the sexes in all previous cultures has been much too strong and has been maintained by a massive use of social and psychological force. If, in a culture that would of necessity be socialist, the ego were to be allowed to develop to its full potential, tension between the sexes would be less sharply divisive in its exterior manifestations but it would not lose its strength. On the contrary, the disappearance of external demarcation lines between the sexes – the taboo on homosexuality, sex differences in clothes, hairstyle, gestures, movement, social behaviour in general – would individualize sex, and relations between the sexes would at last be humanized.

[26] Peter Furth and Herbert Marcuse: 'Emanzipation der Frau in der repressiven Gesellschaft' ('The Emancipation of Women in Repressive Society') in *Das Argument*, no. 23, 1963, p. 10.

# Chapter 6

# Defensive Action against
# Repressive Desublimation

Defensive action is at once a political concept and a psychological one. The liberating aspect is differently defined in the two cases. As a political concept it implies combative action taken by the ruled against 'infringements' by the rulers, in situations where they have become so unused to making their material interests felt that they limit the class conflict to defending themselves against the most extreme manifestations of ruling class power, without undertaking any continuous or thought-out action against the whole system which produces such 'infringements'.

Individual defensive struggles are often exclusively directed towards the preservation of elitist privileges for the protesting group, and not for an improvement in the social position of the whole class.

They can only be accounted wholly positive if they take place within the context of a political movement: a party or at least a loose political organization. It is this that establishes a liberating dimension to what was previously only defensive action. The political mediation has a psychological counterpart. Under fascism the working masses were not only physically robbed of their leadership and deprived of their organization. They were robbed of the *collective ego ideal* they possessed in the pre-fascist era. The class-consciousness of the workers' movement, and the support that it had even among the masses not permanently or actively involved in its organizations, were only the 'conscious' expression of this ego ideal. It gave them the ability to react to the proposals and promises of Marxism in the face of oppression and ever-recurring defeat, not with resignation, but with defiance, strength and solidarity. It found its collective expression in the knowledge that 'we will win in the end, in spite of everything.' This conviction gave the workers the strength to stand up to all the 'temporary' victories of capitalism. By idealizing their own group, and the content of their lives, they protected themselves against the disparaging attitude of the ruling class, which always justified its exploitation and political oppression of the working class by attributing the workers with a quasi-biological incapacity for civilization, and thus denying them any real existence as human beings.

In the years before fascism, these ideals disintegrated step by step. Their decline can be traced in the changes in the proletarian family situation, as well as the upbringing of children within the family, in splitting tactics on the part of the workers' organizations and in the increasingly unreal radical tone of the slogans on banners and leaflets. But leaflets, banners and demonstrations continued to bear witness to the ideals of the workers' movement; they were still there, though the period in which they had been able to take root and flourish – the fifty years of visibly triumphant development for the workers' movement from 1880 to 1930 – was over. This ego ideal was not strong enough to stand up to fascism. But when one considers the psychological and economic resources that the fascist movement was able to call upon, which the workers' movement, for structural reasons, had no access to at all, it is a remarkable achievement that the ego ideal of the workers' movement held out against fascism for as long as it did.

The ego ideal is not to be identified with the super-ego. It is rather a function of the super-ego, which can only be developed on the basis of a relatively independent ego which is not torn between super-ego and id. Freud writes about the super-ego:

It is also the vehicle of the ego ideal by which the ego measures itself, which it emulates, and whose demand for ever greater perfection it strives to fulfil. There is no doubt that this ego ideal is the precipitate of the old picture of the parents, the expression of admiration for the perfection which the child then attributed to them.[1]

Admiration of parental perfection is a wholly adequate and rational attitude for a young child in that it encourages him or her to become autonomous. The child's damaged narcissism is restored by the knowledge of its parents' strength, while it learns at the same time to sublimate its narcissistic instincts. If in later life this infantile admiration for the parents is not simply carried over onto other, more extended, sources of authority, but is transformed and redirected onto qualitatively new ideals, in accordance with the individual's adult personality, the super-ego which evolves these ideals has a positive function in the person's private and social orientation: this function is the ego

---

[1] Freud: *Dissection of the Personality*, no. xxxi of the *New Introductory Lectures on Psycho-Analysis*, 1933 (1932), op. cit., vol. XXII, pp. 64–5.

ideal. The internalized party apparatus which makes up the super-ego of a typical Communist or Social Democrat official derives from the fact that the person concerned carried over his admiration for his parents directly onto an equally dependent admiration for the authority of the party; the infantile and imperfect qualities of dependent admiration have never been overcome. It would be more correct in this case to talk about obedience to authoritarian norms. The super-ego has no need of an ego ideal to carry out this kind of function, and in any case, it is not characteristic of behaviour of this sort that the ego feels spurred on to ever increasing perfection. This feeling was very much present in the idealism of the workers' movement: their *solidarity*, the purpose of which was to overcome dependence on authority; their *discipline*, which they imposed on themselves collectively, in the knowledge that the individual was still weak; their *consciousness of future victory* which was the collective expression of the striving for perfection; their *communist utopia*, the concrete model of perfection. It is clear that these aims were only imperfectly fulfilled. Otherwise when the workers' organizations were liquidated, the collective ego ideal of its members would not have been so completely, and above all so quickly destroyed. That this ego ideal could not even begin to be rebuilt after fascism demonstrates all too clearly the extent to which physical organization and the mental developments of ideals are intertwined. In our present age, this is an extremely gloomy consideration.

The ego ideal is in certain respects nearer to the ego than the super-ego. If we study the conditions in which it exists, it becomes evident that ideally the super-ego arises *out of* the ego and is not imposed on it from without. The latter seems to be becoming more and more frequently the case in the present-day formation of the super-ego. The ego ideal is immediately responsible for formulating the functions that the ego has to perform; achievements in knowledge and awareness, control of reality, control and distribution of instinctual drives, etc. In this respect, the quality of the ego ideal, in contrast to the quality of the super-ego, depends directly upon the strength of the ego.

In *Autorität und Familie* Erich Fromm stated that the development of the ego was closely connected to the position of the individual within the power structure: 'The ruling class has the broadest conspectus of society, and when it is at the height of its power, its members have the most highly developed egos.' This statement has been proved to be correct, but the sociological hypothesis which he proceeded to draw from it about the development of society is only partially so. The negative side of his conclusions has been substantiated, the positive has not. 'The deeper that social differences become, and the less the ruling order fulfils its social obligation in a rational and progressive way, the less does its rule become conducive to the formation of a strong ego.' This function will then pass to other social groups. By 'other social groups', Fromm, writing in 1936, still meant the proletariat, which he thought would come into power and take on the most valuable parts of the ego-development of its predecessor, the bourgeoisie, as culturally objectivized. This would in turn further the development of their own collective ego.

Fromm's assumption that the intended socialist revolution would run on the same lines, so far as emotional and socio-psychological factors were concerned, as the bourgeois revolution had done before it, has proved to be too simple a view. I will not go into a detailed critique of the view that 'socially acquired ego-qualities are inherited by the revolutionary class', since in previous chapters I have already done this in my discussion of specialized aspects of social and psychological life, which seemed to me to demonstrate that a general disintegration of ego-qualities is going on throughout society. In contemporary late-capitalist society, methods of stabilizing socio-economic power are beginning to come into force whereby rulers and ruled can have quite feeble egos, without the system of domination falling apart. In positive terms, the ruling class has lost some of the traditional ego-abilities built up by its forebear, the rising bourgeoisie; but in spite of this – and partly *because* of it[2] – it is still strong enough to take care that the objectivized results of its bygone ego-achievements do not pass over to the other classes. If this were to happen, it would certainly lose its power. An economic result of this method of ensuring the continuance of power in the same hands, which has strong social implications, is that a considerable part of the intellectual resources already acquired by society are repressed, or not developed, or at the very least not given their proper social due. This particularly includes the creative ego-abilities. In other words, a great many opportunities for gratification, which could have been put into effect long ago, such as social innovations, and the rationalization of work processes – especially at the lower economic levels – are suppressed. This is a price which has to be paid, because

[2] If it had not been for the collective loss of qualities such as honesty, humanity, bourgeois tolerance and sensitivity, the ruling class could never have perpetrated the collective barbarism of the Vietnam war.

were these possibilities developed, were it even perhaps admitted that they need not remain in their present stunted form for ever, the reproduction of the characteristic social relations of late capitalism would be seriously endangered.

In these societies the ego-achievements demanded of the upper middle class are in general the norm against which all social classes are measured. The same goes for the criteria of sexual behaviour which determine what is a criminal offence and what punishment should be meted out for it. It is in itself repressive that the norms should be drawn from so limited a field. This is especially demonstrated by the I Q tests used to ascertain achievement potential. Although the standards for these tests are drawn up by analysing middle-class subjects, they are applied indifferently to all members of the population. And the I Q test only measures the 'socially useful' aspects of an individual's capacity for achievement, in particular the qualities required for the middle-class professions. It has been empirically proved that I Q tests take little account of creativity, and great account of retentive memory. It is thus inevitable that working-class people cannot come up to the required standard, and that while the I Q test remains the only accepted selection system they are bound to remain at a disadvantage and their underprivileged economic condition will be reinforced. The middle class thus has a part in the exercise of social domination in that its typical social and psychological attributes are used as a general norm for the whole of society.

The lower classes do register this vaguely in that they recognize, in a resigned fashion, that they are in a subordinate position. Their resentment of, and resistance to, manifestations of political opposition by middle-class people (students, intellectuals, 'layabouts') as the pranks of young aristocrats still contains the slight suggestion of an orientation towards an ego ideal. But the core of this resistance is an ossified adherence to the old middle-class norms. It would be more correct to describe this as a rigid orientation towards the middle-class super-ego than as a collective lower-class ideal. Their techniques of defensive action bear a strong resemblance to collective psychotic (wildly projective and regressive) defence mechanisms, which is only the psychological expression of a contemporary form of false consciousness. For in this kind of action they are in fact throwing in their lot with the wrong side, in that the qualities they are implicitly supporting are hard work, compulsion and obedience, which even express the middle classes. The middle class are dominated, in one respect, just as much as the lower class, since in their case as well it is only *certain* ego-qualities that are tolerated, encouraged, and rewarded.

But the lower classes are the greatest sufferers. They have even less opportunity for establishing a personal (albeit repressive) ego-identity – and without this no collective ego ideal can be formed. This situation is particularly clearly described in Heide Berndt's essay on 'The Sociogenesis of Psychiatric Illness'. The American lower class has a higher incidence of psychotic breakdown (especially schizophrenia) than any other social class. On the basis of this discovery Heide Berndt voices the question, implicit in American empirical psychiatric literature as a whole: why does the adoption of roles in American lower-class families so resemble a 'compulsively neurotic collective defence mechanism'?[3] One of the conclusions that she draws from this is that members of the lower class, in their attempts to succeed socially and economically, have to adopt the values of the middle class. But the lower-class system of norms, and of child rearing, on the basis of which it tries to build up its future role, is subordinate to the corresponding middle-class systems. The people concerned are more likely to suffer psychotic breakdown in the pursuit of their goal, because they have been inadequately trained for middle-class norms, which bear no relation to their actual circumstances; they *force themselves* into a mould which does not fit them. 'When these people deviate into psychosis, it seems as though they have been broken by attempting to tackle class differences on their own. Regrettably, individual attempts to tackle the differences are the rule; none are made on the collective plane.'

If one translates 'class differences' into 'class barriers' and 'collective plane' into 'class struggle', and moves the field of the

---

[3] Of course the working class are not rigidly attached to middle-class norms in all late-capitalist countries, and in none of them are they entirely so. Even in the USA, where this process seems to be farthest advanced, there are examples of the opposite state of affairs, though it would seem truer to describe these as remnants of a previous state than as the beginnings of a new class consciousness. Thus Peter Marris, discussing the social aspect of living conditions, writes about a well-integrated lower-class area which was declared a 'slum' and demolished: 'If this were all, the subculture would be as dreary as it seems to many conventional observers – apathetic, conformist, leaderless, intolerant, frightened, and quasi-criminal. But its countervailing ethic is free, too, to emphasize the virtues most difficult to reconcile with American norms – it places loyalty above ambition, solidarity above competition, personal relationships above impersonal goals, open-handedness above thrift, and the enjoyment of the present above care for the future.'

action – making the necessary modifications – to West Germany, or to any other late capitalist country where a similar tendency is in operation – it becomes clear how central a concept the ego ideal is. It will probably be objected that, in pre-fascist times too, middle-class norms were the standard for the lower class, and that if a lower-class person wanted to succeed, he too would have to make an individual, purely personal, attempt to comply with them. This is true. Wilhelm Reich and other theoreticians of the workers' movement were constantly complaining that the proletarian family worked just like the petty-bourgeois family as an 'ideology factory'. Why then have psychotic breakdowns in lower-class families risen to such an extraordinary level in this generation?

In the previous era the working class could, at least partially, oppose their own ideal of working-class values to the normative compulsion exercised by the system's middle-class ideals. Although these values had only very inadequate access into the proletarian family, it was recognized at work that 'the wheels stop turning, if you decide to stop them'. The stabilizing effect of this ideal on working-class social identity and mental health cannot be overestimated. When this principle really grew naturally out of a collective ego ideal, and was not imposed from without as an authoritarian super-ego, it released powerful forces of class struggle. Socialist organizations like *Rote Hilfe* ('Red Aid') or *Internationale Arbeiterhilfe* ('International Workers' Aid') were probably better able to take on the function of developing the collective ego ideal in the years before fascism than were the party and trade-union apparatus, because they were closer to the immediate needs of the masses than the latter, which, through their loss of contact with the masses, had become all too inflexible and authoritarian in their stance. Movements like Sexpol were organized for this very reason. The collective ego ideal set effective and positive defence mechanisms in motion in the service of political goals, and against collective neurosis. But it was not strong enough to deal with fascism, which can from this point of view be described as a collective neurosis – even if its exact nature as such as not yet understood. Fascism forced its way into power in the face of all defence mechanisms erected by reason and put up pathological defence mechanisms in their place, which did not depend on the individual ego but on a collective super-ego.

Of course the workers in the pre-fascist period were still in such a subordinate position that they had to artificially limit the scope of their egos, in order to be able to build up any ideal at all.

Not only were they economically underprivileged – as were the petty-bourgeoisie – but what was more, they were socially underprivileged. A member of the lower classes was defined *a priori*, in his own eyes and those of others, as a proletarian. This situation explains the narrowness of the ideals which the workers' movement persuaded the proletariat to adopt. It was a necessary condition for the formation of a collective ego ideal under extremely unfavourable social circumstances, however harmful its later effects have turned out to be.

These social circumstances deteriorated so much during fascism and afterwards, that one cannot say that the subordinate classes in present-day West Germany have even the beginnings of a collective ego ideal. How far the intellectual opposition and the radical young will develop a collective ego ideal cutting across all class barriers, and thus form a new 'cultural opposition', remains as yet an open question. In any case the foundations are being laid at this moment with the widening of the protest movement.

In psychoanalytic theory the concept of *defence* has only recently come in for systematic consideration. The chief reason for this is that the role of the ego and its multiple defensive activities against neurotic and especially psychotic illness was only recognized at a very late stage. We have to thank Anna Freud in particular for this addition to our field of knowledge. She takes up a statement thrown out by Freud, but not further developed by him:

In an appendix to *Inhibitions, Symptoms and Anxiety* (1926) Freud reverted to an old concept of defence, stating that he thought it would undoubtedly be an advantage to use it again 'provided we employ it explicitly as a general designation for all the techniques which the ego makes use of in conflicts which may lead to a neurosis, while we retain the word "repression" for that special method of defence which the line of approach taken by our investigations made us better acquainted with in the first instance'. Here we have direct refutation of the notion that repression occupies a unique position amongst psychic processes, and a place is made in psycho-analytic theory for others which serve the same purpose, namely 'the protection of the ego against instinctual demands' . . . Were it not for the intervention of the ego or of those external forces which the ego represents, every instinct would know only one fate – that of gratification. To these nine methods of defence which are very familiar in the practice and have been exhaustively described in the theoretical writings of psycho-analysis (regression, repression, reaction-formation, isolation, undoing, projection, introjection, turning against the self and reversal) we must add a tenth, which pertains rather to the study of the normal than to that of neurosis: sublimation, or displacement or instinctual aims.

So far as we know at present the ego has these ten different methods at its disposal in conflicts with instinctual representatives and affects. It is the task of the practising analyst to discover how far these methods prove effective in the processes of ego-resistance and symptom-formation which he has the opportunity of observing in individuals.[4]

We could go further and say that it is the task of sociological and political analysis to discover which of the techniques that would enable the ego to put up a fight are no longer developed, which are being reduced or deformed, which play the greatest role at present, and what collective symptoms and mental illnesses result.

The individual ego comes into existence through a process of delimitation: it is 'extruded' from the id. Its genesis in the id determines an important function retained lifelong by the adult ego. Anna Freud writes: 'The danger which threatens the ego is that it may be submerged by the instincts; what it dreads above all is the "quantity" of instinct. . . . The defensive measures which its dread of the strength of the instincts impels it to adopt are designed to maintain this differentiation between ego and id, and to ensure the permanence of the newly established ego-organization.'[5] The ways in which this task is fulfilled or not fulfilled are best studied when the struggles of the ego to prevent itself from being swamped by the instincts result in psychosis and perversion. In this case the ego itself is in an over-stimulated condition. Individuals who suffer under such conflicts have insufficient techniques to control their instincts from within, and they react to 'sudden' controls and denials from the outside world, or from their own partially developed super-ego, with exaggerated defensive techniques: total regression and flight from reality, or splitting of the ego. A possible result of this is psychosis or perversion. People in this position fall back on defence mechanisms which cannot really be said to be a function of the ego, since they do not protect it, but destroy or split it.

It should be noted that being submerged by the instincts is not an always existent danger, emanating from the id, against which a healthy person is simply better able to defend himself than someone who becomes mentally ill. An important part of what is subjectively experienced as danger consists of internalized factors

[4] Anna Freud: *The Ego and the Mechanisms of Defence*, pp. 46–7.
[5] Anna Freud: op. cit., p. 181.

from the socio/cultural world outside which have taken up residence in the super-ego. The process is that the super-ego first interprets the tendency in the id to the whole of the psyche as a danger, and reacts with fear, then passes on to the ego the task of mobilizing defence mechanisms against this fear. From this we can draw the conclusion that the task of warding off the instincts is only partially undertaken in the interests of the ego, and that the other, possibly even larger part of the process, is undertaken by the ego in the interests of the super-ego. Anna Freud has scarcely gone into this question at all. As she so rightly pointed out, a significant gap was left in early psychoanalytic theory and practice by its failure to take account of anything but the behaviour of the id, and the reactions of the super-ego, but she has only gone half way to filling it. Though she rightly lays stress on the function of the ego in analysis and in everyday life, she neglects the relationship between the ego and the super-ego or the ego ideal. In fact in the course of her research she even comes to equate the (healthy) ego with the super-ego.

This failure to distinguish sufficiently between ego and super-ego occurs in the work of other writers, who, contrary to Anna Freud, are predominantly sociological in their orientation. Fromm[6] argues as if there were a reciprocal mechanical relationship between ego and super-ego, on the assumption that authority and super-ego are of necessity bound, and that the super-ego has to go on being constantly re-established by real and powerful sources of authority. He concludes from this that, if education were to become more rational, if society (outside world and its norms) were also to become rational and provide a great amount of real gratification for its members, then the super-ego would in the process gradually lose more and more of its significance. But this is only true for the most archaic forms of super-ego, those that belong in a world where feeling and thought are very primitive. It is true that as society becomes more irrational, the super-ego and its functions become more irrational also, and above all more inflexible, and that the autonomy of the ego is thereby reduced. But the obverse conclusion is not valid.

Similarly, M. D. Eder, writing in the *Internationale Zeitschrift für Psychoanalyse* for 1929, identified the super-ego too strongly with its main contemporary function, that of internalizing irrational authority and mobilizing fear against the id. He had

[6] In *Autorität und Familie*, op. cit., p. 86.

the growing impression 'that the individual would not be forced into the compromise of a neurotic character or neurotic symptoms if instincts emanating from the id could be controlled by something less rigid and more adaptable, and thus more realistic, than the super-ego'. In opposition to the idea of a rigid super-ego legitimizing itself 'through a moral code or attitudes inherited from the distant past', Eder set up the vision of a rational society in which the super-ego is done away with by the ego which originally brought it forth. He saw in the 'disappearance of control by the super-ego and its replacement by control by the ego, a more hopeful line of advance for the individual and even for the whole race'.

This construct is a very alluring one for any progressive social theory. And indeed, the fact that today's repressive society has produced an exactly opposite result lends credence to the theory rather than otherwise. Our society has produced a decrease in autonomous ego-functions and their replacement by a super-ego that can be steered by manipulation. This tendency has been termed, among other things, 'collective weakening of the ego', meaning that the ego has an increasing tendency to give up its independence *vis-à-vis* the super-ego, and to put itself in a position where it is unconditionally at the service of the super-ego.

One must tread carefully here, as there are several possible misunderstandings that can arise at this point, and not only because of difficulties of terminology. Neither the ego nor the super-ego, as determining powers in the personality, should be regarded as identical with the functions that individuals employ to control reality. It can be said of the weak ego that it can comprehend certain of the means at its disposal for controlling reality only in a rudimentary way or through the mirror of outside influences, and that it has therefore largely forfeited the *qualities* of independence and power to order opposing or uncoordinated instincts. But it does not completely lose such qualities. Instead it builds up other functions, which from the healthy point of view are neurotic or psychotic. This does not mean however that the person necessarily behaves in a manifestly neurotic or psychotic way according to the social definition of mental illness. The majority of so-called well-adjusted and integrated individuals in present-day society may well employ defensive ego-functions which according to Anna Freud belong more to neurosis than normality (regression, undoing, reversal). Indeed without the predominance of these techniques, the dominant 'normal' way of interpreting political and social events would be impossible. But this does not mean that the ego is tending to disappear; it means that some of the traditional qualities of the ego, which have evolved historically and been handed on from one generation to the next, and whose proper use would have made such techniques superfluous, undergo an involution and a mutilation.

The same structural differentiation exists in the case of the super-ego. In describing an individual's super-ego, one might term it, according to its predominant qualities, criminal, authoritarian, rigid, partial, fragmented or externalized; one would not however say that *all* super-egos were automatically authoritarian, irrational or rigid, and could cease to be so when united with the ego. In the same way, one can differentiate between various functions of the super-ego; for example, reminding the individual of social values (introjection of social norms, in some circumstances by means of introjection of personal authorities), establishing a feed-back mechanism in relation to deviations from those norms (conscience); forming ideals, which the ego will follow in developing its qualities and functions (development of an ego ideal). Only on this basis can one critically analyse a large number, or possibly even the majority of the qualities that the super-ego possesses in society, and the functions it performs, and decide whether, in an achieved rational society, it should be neglected or done away with. (Though it must not be forgotten that in order to *achieve* a social situation different from the present one people would have to struggle and possibly even give their lives, which would demand a very high degree of development of one function of the super-ego, namely, to help bring forth an ego ideal!)

In assessing the super-ego the following questions would be relevant. Which instincts emanating from the id are suppressed, and with what results for the individual? Is any account taken of the ego and if so what? Does the super-ego cooperate with it or weaken it? Does, for example, the ego lose any desirable qualities (autonomous control of reality) through authoritarian or manipulative action on the part of the super-ego? What defensive action does it force the ego to adopt? Is this rationally acceptable from the point of view of social development, how strong is the defensive action, and what effect does it have on the ego?

From what we have seen so far, it appears likely that a really healthy individual who is fully capable of dealing with reality mainly uses the super-ego to form ideals. The predominant function of the ego is to mediate, not to make value judgements. Looking forward to an ideal social and individual situation it seems as though the ego and the ego ideal would cooperate as follows. The ego ideal, developed out of primary narcissism and responsible to it would describe *what* should be done; the ego would decide *how* it should be done, submitting the techniques it uses to the ego ideal *and* the id for confirmation. The ego would have reconquered the super-ego, and its function would be at once concrete, and utopian.

This form of cooperation between ego and super-ego is also the general precondition for all forms of sublimation. This does not mean that repression, the alternative to sublimation, is not equally the product of joint action by ego and super-ego; but the situation then is quite different. Repression is undertaken by the ego at the command of the super-ego, which is not obliged, in cases of doubt, to justify its demands to the ego. But it is insufficient to describe sublimation as simply the displacement of an instinct onto an objective different from its basic one. This would not make it definitively different from repression. In the case of sublimation the emphasis lies on *where* the instinct is displaced to, and with what results for the individual. In the case of repression the instinct is *pushed out of sight* into the id, with the result that it has to find another field for its activities. It is then generally out of the individual's control, and can, in certain circumstances, do more harm than the original instinct. But sublimation ultimately results in an actual change, not only of the objective of an instinct, but of the instinct itself. In fact the latter change is the most important; the actual objective can sometimes be retained. The instinct is either turned to the service of the outside world (socially useful activities) or to the service of the ego (narcissism). When we ask 'what the results are', we are also noting what benefit the transformation of an instinct has had for an individual's psyche. One can for example meet people who put all their energies into the service of the 'community', thus appearing to have sublimated personal instincts into social activity; and yet one can see that their sexual and aggressive instincts have not been sublimated but only repressed, with the result that the people concerned suffer under their 'altruism' or 'idealism', which are simply the escape routes for repressed aggressive and anal-sadistic drives.

After these remarks on sublimation, it seems very inadequate to set up 'sublimation or displacement of the goal of an instinct' as the only method by which a healthy individual can defend himself against fear of reality or fear of his own instincts, when

Anna Freud listed nine methods which the neurotic and the psychotic, but also, in proportionately smaller measure, the healthy individual can use to defend himself. The mental health of an individual and his capacity for coping with reality do not after all depend on his capacity for sublimating his instincts, but on his ability to do justice to the demands of the id and the outside world. If we want to retain Anna Freud's schema, we have to extend the concept of sublimation to cover everything pertaining to the control of reality, the instincts and the super-ego. For with reference to the danger of being submerged by the instincts another point needs to be added, namely that this is *not only* a function of insufficient ego controls (capacity for sublimation in healthy people, necessity for repression in the mentally unhealthy) but also of the degree of instinctual liberty that a society has at its disposal, the number of forms that this liberty can take, and the degree of tolerance the society shows towards those of its members who deviate. If one widens the concept of sublimation so far, it loses its specific technical meaning as one of the defence mechanisms employed to protect the ego. But this more limited definition is a useful one to retain for the time being, however, in making clear the extent of what *repressive* or *controlled desublimation* means for the individual.

The *adult* individual in the psychoanalytic sense, i.e. one who is capable of controlling and changing reality, decides on the basis of his ego capacities not only what his attitude is to be to the outside world (institutions and norms of society) but also what his attitude is to be to his sexual and aggressive instincts. In order to decide on the admissability or inadmissability of wishes or acts relating to those instincts, he is just as much in need of the interpretations of his super-ego (or ego ideal) as he is in the case of decisions relating to the outside world. This capacity develops at the same time as his ego. For this reason, it is sometimes said that 'sublimation becomes impossible once one has become an adult'. This description is somewhat imprecise in as much as, though childhood is the time when, in addition to the development of the ego/super-ego relationship, the die is also cast as to whether the child will later dispose of the capacity and techniques for sublimating his instinctual drives, this is a different thing from his character structure, which will later be in charge of the application of these techniques, and which only becomes relatively fixed when adulthood is reached.

The development of the faculty for sublimation – in the sense of all rational and ego-widening forms of control over reality and the instincts – should not be seen as excluding other techniques of defence. The individual who later in life is able, without harm to himself, to make sexual and aggressive instinctual desires 'socially' useful does not learn this capacity in childhood to the exclusion of other techniques of defence; he builds it on top of them. He must 'at some time' have been so weak that he was unable to do without the techniques of repression, of undoing, of reversal, etc., in protecting himself against being submerged by his instincts and interpreting the dangers and denials of the outside world. And in later life he is constantly obliged to return to these techniques of self-protection, at least while the forces of the outside world remain hostile to ego and id. The important thing is that, when the child's ego is in the process of developing, one or more of the infantile protective mechanisms does not gain the upper hand to such a degree that he finds it difficult later to learn other methods of controlling his instincts and reality. If it does, the way in which he transforms his instincts and his perception of the outside world is bound to have a tinge of neurosis or psychosis, and in extreme cases he himself will become neurotic or psychotic.

Repressive and controlled desublimation is the description given to a social situation in which the level of sublimation already attained by that culture is lowered, individual sublimation is collectively broken down, and the faculty for it ceases to be developed except in a rudimentary way. This does not only mean that sexual and aggressive instincts which were previously subjected to a 'social' metamorphosis are 'set free', to be sexualized or to find a manifestly aggressive outcome if so desired. It means above all the decomposition of the ego-achievements. These were what enabled the individuals to exercise personal control over his instincts, to decide which he must repress, which he must transform, and which he can allow free play; and when they decompose, the individual is obliged to abdicate this responsibility. It passes into the hands of the same powers which engineered his desublimation, and they henceforth decide for him how he is to behave from moment to moment, when and how he reacts in an openly sexual way, and when and how he curbs or gives free rein to aggressive urges. The young person, and later the adult, no longer learns to differentiate between instincts that will help or harm the ego, or even between those that are sexual and those that are aggressive. He ceases to be able to decide which to allow, and manipulative forces outside himself take over the decision-making function for him.

The basis of this change lies in a transformation of the defensive mechanisms available to the ego, which regress to an infantile stage of action and reaction. The ego loses most of its classic function of mediating between id, super-ego and outside world and undergoes an involution to a stage at which it simply acts as an agency for the internalization of external authority and compartmentalized influences from the super-ego. With the collective decomposition of the function of the ego, a monopolization takes place in the mechanisms of domination. In psychological terms, the super-ego and ego become one; in political terms, institutionalized techniques of social and political oppression become one with the individual. Desublimation resembles sublimation in so far as it is a way of using the instincts for *social* ends; it is the currently dominant form of socialization.

In this context the concept of defensive action takes on a new meaning. The defensive techniques of the ego can now no longer play a simply conservative or system-stabilizing role; they have to take on a revolutionary role. They now not only have the task of warding off anti-social and personally destructive instinctual urges previously fulfilled by the 'ten' traditional defence mechanisms. They also have to protect the ego from tendencies to repressive desublimation emanating from the collective and externalized super-ego (for example, sexualization through pseudo-genital norms) which form an unholy alliance with the infantile component instincts. There are at least the beginnings of this situation here and there. For psychoanalytic theory and practice, as for the political struggle, it is something rather new. The externalized and fragmented super-ego could be said to have joined forces with the infantile entities of the id to form a common front against the ego. The ego is all the more likely to be defeated in the ensuing conflict, in that its own lack of effective integration is only the obverse of the unintegrated instincts of the much stronger id.

# Chapter 7

# Current Problems of
# Defensive Action

It is a difficult political and psychological undertaking to find a new range of defence mechanisms to complement, and in some cases replace, the classic mechanisms developed by the ego to combat fear of the instincts and of reality, and the moral and political norms justifying them. Moreover, such a proceeding would probably not contribute much to the solution of the problem under consideration, namely, defensive action for combating repressive desublimation. For this reason, all we propose to do here is to discuss various already existing models of political and psychological defensive action. The relative success or failure of these in improving individual ego-integration and democratizing society will make clear what are the difficulties facing those who are fully or even unconsciously aware of the current social tendency to controlled desublimation, and are engaged in the struggle against it.

## 'TOTAL SEXUAL FREEDOM'

The most modern variants of bourgeois sexual reform come from Sweden, the capitalist welfare state *par excellence*. Nowhere else do sexual taboos and repression carry so little weight in social norms and the law, nowhere else has individual sexual education become so much a matter for the community, no other place has a greater traditional concern for the bourgeois freedom of the individual, and for the protection of political, racial and sexual minorities. *The Sexual Minorities* by Lars Ullerstam provides the clearest illustration of a tendency in capitalist countries, which its proponents see as radical and progressive, to permit any kind of human or human/animal sexual manifestations, to regard them all as equal, and to encourage their occurrence, even down to acts involving physical cruelty to people and animals. We intend here only to discuss Ullerstam's suggestions for sexual reform, but what we say about them can be taken to cover other works of a similar nature, if not perhaps quite so 'uncompromising', 'unprejudiced' and 'progressive' as his.

Ullerstam starts from the empirically and theoretically sound assumption that no sexual behaviour should be illegal, except rape, incest, and in some cases intercourse with minors. So far his suggestions for reform are acceptable and right. But this is not the core of his book. His basic proposition is that everyone possessed by a manifestly perverted, neurotic, infantile or regressive instinct should be allowed – without regard to what his particular deviation is – to 'work it off' and gain as much enjoyment in the process as possible. To this purpose a whole network of arrangements should be set up to gratify the various needs. In his view, *every* division in sexual matters between 'normal' and 'abnormal' or 'unhealthy' is only a matter of definition, the defining agencies being at present the state, the church and popular morality. If this could be done away with, an optimum of individual happiness would almost automatically come into being:

Certain masturbators specialize in writing 'dirty words' in edifying books. . . . All one can say is that they have found a harmless method of gratification. An author ought to be grateful that he was able to provide such a pleasure for some of his fellow human beings. . . .

Urophiles hang about public lavatories, and their greatest desire is to find someone who will be obliging enough to urinate in their hats or pockets. . . . The need to have one's clothing fouled with urine is doubtless not a very elevated one, but it is horrifying to hear people boasting about having maltreated these individuals. Even if one does not wish to give in to these people's humble desire, one ought at least to be polite to them. . . . Brothels would save the unmarried man, at any rate if he were highly sexed, a lot of time which he could devote to his education. Sexually exhausted wives could send off their husbands to the brothel without fear of complications, and take a well-earned rest. A visit to a brothel would be a natural and healthy way to work off the sexual excitement provoked by the erotic parties and dances which our society is so given to. People's enjoyment of parties would no longer be disturbed by the frantic search for somebody to go to bed with. . . .

Let us improve the pornographic service! Voyeurs ought not to have to sit through hours of *The Silence* and such like depressing material just to catch the vaguest hint of a coitus scene. . . . There ought to be films showing masturbation, heterosexual intercourse, lesbian activities, sodomy, group sex and so on, to cater for different tastes. It would be a good idea if some cinemas were so arranged that people could masturbate in the auditorium.

This model of a multi-form system of gratification is an example of economic efficiency via pseudo-gratification: social regulation of conflicts *and* sexual manipulation, combined in one. Such phrases as 'no complications', 'healthy way to work off . . .', 'time to devote to his education' and 'no longer disturbed by' are typical of the parlance of techno/economic efficiency. It is actually the last, most radical example which demonstrates most clearly that the gratification being offered is only an *institutionalization* of sexual pseudo-gratification. In point of fact it is a characteristic of the voyeur's perversion that it cannot do without permanent sexual tension, and it is highly likely that a large number of perverts would probably prefer *The Silence* as a sexual stimulus to unambiguously pornographic films, while the rest would only fall into a routine of abnormal behaviour which would cut down their awareness of their subjective misery, and with it their chances of coming to understand their illness and possibly being cured. The same is true of the forms of masturbation related to infantile and regressive compulsions. Ullerstam never once even hints that it might be better if the social system could be altered in such a way that the majority of neuroses and perversions would lose their reason for existence, and would only emerge occasionally, as marginal phenomena, which would then be treated individually, or if this proved impossible, be accorded a maximum of tolerance, and the possibility for gratification. This would be a revolutionary attitude to sexuality, if a rather abstract one. He does not even say that perversions which cause the people afflicted with them nothing but misery and frustrated despair should be clinically treated. He intends society and its perverts to remain as they are, with society creating institutions for the care of the perverted on the welfare state principle so successfully employed elsewhere.

In individual proposals of Ullerstam's one can still see traces of the great bourgeois-revolutionary programme: the greatest happiness of the greatest number. It is these traces which make his individual proposals so similar – to the point of interchangeableness – to those of the left, particularly the anti-authoritarian movements among young people and intellectuals. This is precisely what makes it a matter of life or death to place every demand in the context of the struggle for individual and political emancipation. If this is not done, all the demands figuring in a programme of social emancipation will sooner or later be drawn into the gravitational field of official gratification, and suffer a repressive transformation. *When* this occurs is simply a matter of the amount of resistance put up by the openly anti-sexual pre-capitalist forces in society against the new forces of repressive desublimation. This can be shown by two examples.

In the USA parts of Ullerstam's programme are already in operation. In the chapter on socially adapted promiscuity we quoted the example of the mail order firm dealing in leather articles 'for lovers of domestic chastisement'. It is only a forerunner of all kinds of specialist businesses catering to different perversions. There are already such shops in the large cities of the USA. Especially popular at present – for reasons inherent in the cultural situation – are the 'Sex and Leather' shops. These not only sell all the leather articles pertaining to that perversion, but lay on cinema shows of pornographic films for their customers in a room at the back of the shop. People are allowed to watch the films for a length of time corresponding to the amount they have spent on books and objects in the shop, after which they are mercilessly driven back into the shop.

Secondly, some of the school groups in the Independent High-School Students Action Centre (AUSS) have demanded the installation of machines dispensing the contraceptive pill in schools. This demand is also considered by its proponents as socially emancipating. It cannot be denied that it does have this aspect, but it is one that can just as easily be turned into its opposite: a repressive compulsion to conform. In the USA the oral contraceptive can be bought in drug stores, and it is probably only a matter of time before this is possible in Germany also. These are the factors that make it tactically impossible to run progressive political campaigns in the USA or Sweden in schools on the basis of such demands as sexual enlightenment. But, more important, they are factors which openly incite people to the adoption of genital behaviour before they have gone through the exacting experiences of being in love, and committing themselves to solidarity and to fidelity which would make them emotionally ready for it. If the pill comes openly into the class-room it will be much less difficult for boys to persuade girls that their fear of coitus is 'stupid'. If they happen to be AUSS members they will even be able to tell a girl who remains recalcitrant in spite of the pill that she is repressive.

The dangers of repressive desublimation, which increase with every widening of the bounds of what is socially permitted in terms of gratification, cannot be done away with by a programme of political asceticism. In any circumstances this would be reactionary. The important thing is to define the exact nature of every specific gratification by making a distinction between 'socially permitted' and 'desirable for the individual'. The only position from which this can successfully be done is that of sublimation based upon a flexible ego ideal. This is what Marcuse means when he says 'In contrast to the pleasures of adjusted desublimation, sublimation preserves the consciousness of the renunciations which the repressive society inflicts upon the individual, and thereby preserves the need for liberation.'[1]

## THE POLITICS OF PUBERTY

Anna Freud has pointed out that young people fend off and finally transform the upsurge of libido that is a physiological characteristic of puberty predominantly by means of two mechanisms: 'asceticism' and 'intellectualization'. These are less evident in the latency period and adulthood, because the instinctual life is normally calmer then, and the ego relatively stronger.[2] There is something compulsive about these mechanisms, as is shown by the fact that the demands of the super-ego which underlie them have an exterior, abstract quality. They can impose themselves with totalitarian force on the individual and then, suddenly, disappear again without any deep character change having occurred.

The intellectualization typical of puberty in its 'classic' form is not, therefore, intellectualism in the ordinary sense. It is much more a direct way of protecting the ego against being submerged, by reinforcing the twin mechanism of 'asceticism'. The young person's behaviour is scarcely touched: 'He evidently derives gratification from the mere process of thinking, speculating or discussing. His behaviour is determined by other factors and is not necessarily influenced by the result of these intellectual gymnastics'.[3] But this form of intellectualization generally has an important side effect on the young person's capacity for dealing with reality after puberty:

If it is true that an increase in libidinal cathexis invariably has the automatic effect of causing the ego to redouble its efforts to work over the instinctual processes intellectually, this would explain the fact that instinctual danger makes human beings intelligent. In periods of calm in the instinctual life, when there is no danger, the individual can permit himself a certain degree of stupidity.[4]

There is no empirical proof that there is a correlation between abstinence and intellectual achievement, despite the frequent

[1] Herbert Marcuse: *One Dimensional Man*, p. 71.
[2] Anna Freud: op. cit., p. 166.
[3] op. cit., p. 176.
[4] op. cit., p. 179.

assertions that are made to the contrary; Freud himself is very definite on this point.[5]

There are inpications that in recent times this process is being reversed. The repressive methods being used to break down the old demands for abstinence are bringing about a collective stupidity. The social tendency to repressive desublimation makes itself felt in puberty chiefly through the permanent, if fragmented, flood of offers of sexualization and gratification which pour in on adolescents from the outside world. Fear of the instincts (that is, of the ego being submerged by the id) is forcibly decreased, and present-day adolescents do not build up the traditional defensive mechanisms to fight it. This is the light in which Marcuse should be understood, when he says: 'In the mental apparatus, the tension between that which is desired and that which is permitted seems considerably lowered and the Reality Principle no longer seems to require a sweeping and painful transformation of instinctual needs. The individual must adapt himself to a world which does not seem to demand the denial of his innermost needs – a world which is not essentially hostile.'[6]

This theoretical prognosis is confirmed in detail by a representative inquiry into young people's attitudes recently carried out in Germany. This seems to indicate that the classic conflicts of puberty no longer take place, or at least, that individuals are not consciously aware of them. Eighty-seven per cent of the ten- to nineteen-year-olds questioned claimed to be 'very happy at home'. The most admired attributes ('ideals' is no longer the word) were smart appearance, stylish and modern clothes, and polite behaviour. Children of ten to fourteen were readily able to name skin and hand creams, the youngest boys were able to name not only one but several brands of lipstick. Even attempts to bring up young people to be good citizens in the system's own terms have not been successful; for example, the older that boys were, the less positive was their attitude to the armed forces. All 'ideals', even those encouraged by the system, are regarded by the young as being too risky. Only conformity to the immediate environment is felt to be safe and profitable. This makes them so

[5] Freud: *'Civilized' Sexual Morality and Modern Nervous Illness*, p. 197: 'In general I have not gained the impression that sexual abstinence helps to bring about energetic and self-reliant men of action or original thinkers or bold emancipators and reformers. Far more often it goes to produce well-behaved weaklings who later become lost in the great mass of people that tends to follow, unwillingly, the leads given by strong individuals.'
[6] *One Dimensional Man*, p. 70.

much the better consumers, as the answers to the question about lipstick shows. From their earliest youth, they are consumer conscious; their social identity seems to derive chiefly from it. This fact is made use of by *Bravo* and other magazines, who were responsible for the inquiry quoted above. In December 1967, *Bravo* had almost daily an advertisement in the *Frankfurter Allgemeine Zeitung*[7] which was worded as follows: 'Products get older with the people who buy them. Products get younger when young people buy them! Speak to them now, and tomorrow they will be your customers!'

Even those young people who are making a serious 'intellectualizing' attempt to break away from the 'happy consciousness' of most of the adult and adolescent world are permanently affected by it. The total incomprehension that they meet with from the others makes their own intellectual development more difficult, and they find themselves driven into a head-on clash, which is made even more violent by the aggression that the 'happy' conformists are permitted to unleash, with society's blessing, on their 'unhappy' opponents. An example of this is the spontaneous wave of mass protest among young people, chiefly still at school or serving an apprenticeship, which was triggered off, apparently rather at random, in February 1968, by the big protests in Bremen against a rise in tram fares, and spread like wildfire to a large number of other towns in West Germany. An interesting factor in these mass protests is that they took place in the very towns in which there was not a strong left-wing student movement to create a political atmosphere or instigate such actions, namely in Bremen, Kiel, Bochum and Hanover.

Anna Freud's judgement on the intellectualizing process typical of the 'classic' form of puberty was 'that these mental performances . . . brilliant and remarkable as they are, remain to a great extent unfruitful'.[8] 'Intellectualizing' movements among young people today seem to be almost conscious of this element of uselessness in their struggle against the tendencies of repressive desublimation. However, it is no longer, as in 'classic' puberty, simply a component part of the defence mechanism against being submerged by the instincts, but a necessary condition of the unhappy consciousness which has to struggle against the dead weight of the 'happy' sector of society, and the batons and hoses of its representatives.

[7] The leading daily newspaper of West German capitalism.
[8] Anna Freud, op. cit., p. 180.

But before this radicalization can become a firm part of the emotional and political struggle against repressive desublimation, it needs to be joined by another factor during the development of the ego in puberty (which is, itself, a process that can only take place today against the stream of social tendencies). This factor is structurally opposed to anything present in the apathy of the majority of today's young people, or in the intellectualizing process of the young people Anna Freud was talking about. It consists of learning that one's radical acts have a reference to oneself; today's young radical minority have to realize, at least emotionally, that their protests have something to do with their own insufficient ego, their own social inferiority, and with their own personal attempts to build up an ego capable of resisting repressive desublimation and opportunistic integration. It is not enough that the batons and hoses of the opposition demonstrate that the enemy exists, and will fight back against their attempts to defend themselves against repressive desublimation. The upsurge of sudden protest actions in an ever increasing number of cities, and the increasing number of young people who transitorily participate in them might lead one to suppose that, though these protest actions are impotent in the sense that they are directed against an overwhelmingly more powerful enemy, yet in an inner, emotional sense they are not so. This would be a mistake. This inner powerlessness will inevitably end by leading to resignation, if the protest movement is only enacted on the political plane, in an escalation of demonstrations, etc. The high degree of fluctuation in young people's support of the movement, the ease with which they become disaffected shows this only too well, even though such actions help to give the political struggle its unremitting character, which protects them from integrative optimism.

To stand as a basis for long-term struggle – not only among the radical minorities now passing through puberty, but also among adults fighting to overcome the compulsion to perpetual puberty – this inner powerlessness has to be supported by an ego ideal which sees in it the power of the powerless, and as such never lets it out of sight. In the political sphere, the most current method of building an ego ideal is to identify with the liberation struggles of the Third World. This, though probably necessary, is not enough. Most students' and young people's identification with the National Liberation Front in Vietnam, with Che Guevara and Mao is only 'external' – rather like the 'intellectualization' typical of 'classic' puberty. Their heroes do not really have the function of ego ideals, though, fortunately, they do not have a rigid super-ego function either. The young people do not really follow their revolutionary models in their lives; they often just grow beards, put on blue tunics, write 'venceremos' under their letters and manifestoes. And at this stage it is a good thing they do not act out the lives of their heroes to the letter, pick up a machine-gun and go out to fight 'imperialism on the home front'. That may become necessary, but the strengthening of one's own ego through orientation to an ego ideal is a basically different process. If one were to take as a model the liberation struggle in the Third World, possible goals in such a process might be to be as cunning and silent in the cities of the imperialist world as the NLF in Vietnam, as brave as Che in Bolivia, as wise as Mao, and so to measure and develop one's own ego qualities. But this has so far seldom been the case.

And yet there is no political alternative to the way in which young people and intellectuals are becoming radicalized. It is tied to the governing form of repression in these countries. In the field of political endeavour, it is the only possibility of fighting collective apathy, conformity, and desublimation. Just as inevitably, even *conformist* young people turn down the possibilities offered them by the existing institutions to build up an ego ideal acceptable to the system. Attempts to turn the young into 'democratic citizens' founder on the reef of repressive desublimation. We have already mentioned their negative attitude to military service. The year of 'social service' which the government has been trying to push for eleven years, and which was intended to develop the ego ideals of the young, has been a dismal failure; no more than a thousand people a year have been volunteering for it, in the whole of West Germany. At a recruiting drive for the social service year, a young man described as typical, reporting on his year of service in a mental hospital, emphasized – at least partially as a proof of the ego ideals developed by the experience – that if one behaved particularly well, after a time one was even given the keys to the medicine cupboard. But one should not fall into the illusion of thinking that conformist youth has an effective super-ego simply because the traditional institutions for fabricating one have lost their power.

The solutions that the traditional left have offered the radical young have up till now been as ineffective as the 'social service year' has been with regard to the conformist majority. The Socialist Centre, for example, in the belief that it can do better than either the SDS on the one hand, or the SPD, DFU[9] and

---

[9] Deutsche Friedens Union: German Peace Union, a left-wing political party

KPD on the other, has been calling on the opposition youth movement not to indulge in such *visibly* radical campaigns, since these will only be misunderstood by sections of the population who would otherwise be progressively inclined, and drive them into the arms of reaction.[10] But their theoreticians have failed to recognize – among other political blind spots – that young people who suffer under the knowledge that the majority of the adolescent and adult population are so 'well-behaved', so inhumanly apathetic, so aggressive (but in ways dictated by society), and would like to fight these defects, cannot be persuaded or disciplined into a mode of conduct which looks to them like obedience, and which would in practice even seem to them to be corrupt and opportunistic. The radical and in part collectively aggressive and regressive acts of the youth and student movements are a problematic – possibly even an ambivalent – weapon in the armoury of the great political struggle against repressive desublimation. Psychologically, they can be described as techniques for defending the ego against hostile outside powers, which also however testify to a weakness within, which they are intended to combat. But they are at present the only possible means for attaining an individual and collective political identity. For this reason they are an indispensable part of the extra-parliamentary political movement, which would break up in a very short time without them.

## THE COMMUNES

The First Commune, which came into being at the end of 1966 in West Berlin, and whose members were excluded from the SDS in May 1967, believes it has evolved a political and organizational form adequate to lead the class struggle in late-capitalist society. It traces its historical antecedents to the youth communes of post-revolutionary Russia, with the condition that it proposes to improve on some of their structural aspects, notably those criticized by Wilhelm Reich,[11] such as their rigid work

---

supported by the West German Communists while their own party was banned.

[10] This was particularly the complaint at the founding conference of the Socialist Opposition held at Offenbach on 3 February 1968. This movement embraces various shades of opinion on the left of the socialist spectrum. The so-called traditional elements of the SDS also belong to it. The conference in question outstripped even the average trade-union meeting in the amount of resentment expressed towards 'the student'.

[11] In *The Sexual Revolution*, pp. 212–34.

orientation, and their repressive sexual morality. Its immediate origins are the groups which formed around *Subversive Aktion* and *Unverbindliche Richtlinien* (Non-Obligatory Principles) in Munich, Stuttgart and Berlin in 1962–3. These groups made yet another attempt at the old task of resolving the contradictions between organization and political practice. The immediate theoretical result was the idea of the 'cohort'. This was conceived as a unified campaign against repressive desublimation – though this idea had not at the time been fully worked out by Marcuse, who was the groups' chief inspiration – which was to be put through *at one blow*:

The development of the whole has to be driven forward at any price, and so the cohort will clear the way for all human possibilities *here and now*. Seeing that it is science that lays down what life is and what its goals are, the cohort proposes a new scientific *doctrine* with a new scale of importance for the sciences. . . . *Subversive Action* is made up of ringleaders of organized disobedience. As a first step towards the emancipated society of the cohort, they declare themselves a pariah élite whose direct purpose is action. The most infinitesimal act has to be judged by the degree to which it lays bare social repression. No one can be part of the subversive left who does not take part actively in the new tradition of revolt. . . .

Since we assume that everyone knows – or ought to know – that it is not enough to have read all the books, we demand a new subversive psyche which will express the subversive state of being. Its genesis: the knowledge of the absolutely undeniable principle of the dialectic, and understanding of the biological law of ambivalence. . . .

Since the development of the whole has to be driven forward at any price, it must be the task of the pariah élite to fight to give all human possibilities room to breathe. . . .

*Subversive Man* keeps his belief in the possibilities of the human, and knows a better world will come; he has seen through the repressive world's attempts to dazzle and hypnotize him. He is a living experiment in all human possibilities – He is *subversive man*. . . . We are going to step onto the stage as heretics and seducers; we have promised the moon out of the sky, but we will get it, and we will keep it!

It is far from our intention to criticize the First Commune for not carrying out these promises. That has been the lot of countless political programmes and communist manifestoes, and it was, after all, disappointment with their predecessors' failure that brought the Commune into being. Nor should one reproach the founders of *Unverbindliche Richtlinien* for not having correctly understood their mentors: Marx, Freud, Adorno. That would be a philological rather than a political criticism. And there are plenty of people around who have understood Marx and Freud correctly and yet so firmly decline to give an answer to the question referred to in this book as 'defensive action against repressive desublimation', that one cannot blame the 'subversives' who have had all too concrete proof of the hopelessness of their endeavour for becoming disenchanted with their work. It seems too much like a convenient way of abdicating from the necessity of direct action, to spend one's whole time – as does for example the Frankfurt School – proclaiming that the dialectic is in an insoluble impasse, and the minute analyses to which the latter submit the work of some of the most vital writers ultimately succeed in making them seem more like the corpse at a post mortem than a living influence. It is also unfair to reproach the First Commune for having jumped on the bandwagon by selling Commune gossip to the illustrated magazines or the television companies, and thus living off the very powers it was claiming to oppose. This criticism can only be applied to some of its less responsible members, and to analyse or criticize them is neither politically edifying nor useful.

The political and personal acts – courageous or outrageous – of the First Commune are well known. I do not intend to add my own commentary on the solutions they have found for emotional and sexual conflicts, to the criticisms already passed on them by bourgeois *and* traditional socialist camps. That these solutions have failed to achieve the desired result can all too easily serve the enemies of the Commune as an easy way of working off their own unconscious aggression and disappointments by projecting their emotional and sexual conflicts onto it. But I am obliged to incur the risk of doing this myself, at least to a small degree. The First Commune has made so many unforgivable political and psychological mistakes that it has failed to produce anything indicative of its original revolutionary intention. And it has promised young people 'the moon out of the sky' for so long, and then so cruelly betrayed and destroyed the hopes which it aroused, that it is essential to criticize it in order to forestall any more such disappointments. What is more, such a critique must be personal, since the Commune set up actual persons as agents of liberation.

The First Commune promised to solve the problems of the weakness of the left with a radically new and original model of organization. The principle of this was that the unbearable tension suffered more or less consciously by all the 'unhappy' members of society, could be wiped out if each individual refused to submit to the compulsion to 'plan for the future' and replaced it by immediate gratification. They opposed the 'Marxist alienation theory' with the concept of 'fun'. And in fact, both these ideas do touch upon structural weaknesses at the heart of the whole anti-authoritarian and anti-capitalist movement. In this the Commune is not different from its numerous anarchist and putschist predecessors, who suffered, and with reason, under the bureaucratic ossification and opportunistic self-castration of the political organizations, broke away from them, but then wrongly decided that political problems would be solved at one blow if the revolutionaries were only to accomplish the revolution completely enough in their own lives. The failure of almost all putschist and anarchist groups can be attributed – when they were not actually liquidated by the forces of the state, or by their party of origin – to the inner resistance which the revolutionaries set up to the demands they made of themselves. A tragic and yet very instructive case of this kind of failure is the fate of Boris Savinkov, the last leader of the fighting organization of the Social Revolutionary Party in Russia.[12]

Taken individually the political and personal acts of the First Commune have done the whole opposition movement as much good as they have harm. It would be quite inappropriate to charge the Commune with individual tactical errors, or with having made the public think that all radical students were bearded, lazy and dirty. They would have thought this anyway, without the help of the Commune: it simply crystallized a prejudice. Nor need the Commune accept the accusation that all along the line it has acted, in the actual struggle, in such a way as to discredit the left-wing movement, prejudice people against it, and set it back a number of steps. The Commune is right to ask whether 'the serious, dreary, useless forests of placards (at traditional demonstrations) were a politically useful measure, and whether, in fact, they did not hinder the so-called cause'. And though it is unfair of the Commune to gloss over all the contradictions in its own position by pointing out the ineffectiveness of the rest of the extra-parliamentary political opposition (including the AStA's[13] and the SDS), it can really only be challenged with being objectively counter-revolutionary if it has failed to fulfil the claim which differentiates it from the rest of the movement: that it has found the key to the problem of a revolutionary existence, and has solved it for its members.

[12] The subject of a novel by Roman Gul, published in England as *General B.O.*, London, 1930.
[13] Allgemeine Studenten Assoziation: the West German General Union of Students.

*Unverbindliche Richtlinien*'s formulation of the problem: 'The key factor which vetoes any attempt at self-realization is the negation of sexuality', if unacceptably bald, is none the less correct. But the answer it gave was wrong: 'The managers' subliminal encroachment on the sexual sphere can only be checked by hard-hitting sexual action. It will be the task of the cohorts to extend this campaign to all spheres of life.' This answer is wrong because repressive desublimation ('subliminal encroachment') builds upon sexual denial within the individual, and on sexual components already 'built into' his character; subliminal encroachment cannot be conquered by campaigns alone, and certainly not at a blow. The First Commune recognized the problem, but its attempt to deal with it was misconceived. The First Commune, and even more its successor, the so-called Second Commune in West Berlin, found that thought was after all necessary as well as action, and organized group sit-ins on the style of psychoanalytic group therapy. But, according to the reports of people who left the Communes, a tendency soon made itself felt which it is difficult to do away with in psychoanalytic group therapy itself: the more psychologically stable (healthy) sector of the group held fast to their own sanity at the cost of the more unstable sector, onto whom they transferred their own repressions and reaction-formations. In a group of young intellectuals this tendency is liable to be even stronger and have even more deadly results because the participants all know something about psychoanalytic theory, and so can 'play at being analysts', but there is no real analyst there who could uncover and break down the repressions and reaction-formations of the stronger half.

The First Commune attempted to set up 'communist' norms for its members and to do away with 'capitalism' for its members here and now. This programme has miscarried. The subjectively revolutionary attitude becomes objectively counter-revolutionary when it leads people to believe that all their hopes can be fulfilled *today*, all their sufferings done away with *today*. The shattering of these hopes has led to many chaotic personal breakdowns among the members of groups founded on the Commune idea throughout West Germany, or, when actual breakdown has been avoided, to deeply resigned attitudes. This process can be discussed in relation to the idea that 'the couple is repressive'. The Commune put forward the idea – not a new one – that *all* exclusive sexual relationships were of necessity repressive, because they resisted the formation of larger, cooperative units. We shall discuss this claim in greater detail in the section on fidelity and marriage. But though it is not sufficient proof that the Commune is wrong in its idea of dissolving the couple into larger, flexible promiscuous units to point out that the units were more repressive than the average couple, and that couples were always falling in love and moving out, the Commune is undeniably wrong to conclude that *all* exclusive relationships (even lifelong ones) are repressive, simply because *in the present historical circumstances* repression is the common denominator of most sexual relationships.

The First Commune wanted to destroy repressive sexual morality. Its alternative however was an abstract morality of liberation which, because individuals did not only suffer from the old morality, but were imbued with it through and through, had to be forced upon them 'here and now'. The communards said: 'We want to stop submitting ourselves to the repression of monogamous marriage and its permitted precursors and studentish surrogates' and instead had to submit themselves to standards of promiscuity for which they had not been psychologically prepared, and under which they therefore necessarily suffered. Their behaviour in one way resembled the asceticism of puberty, in that they submitted themselves to an abstract rule, which they are incapable of keeping up, because it does not conform to their ego/id structure, but is simply imposed from without. The interior results are as terroristic as might be expected. If a tenth of what they say in interviews is to be believed, it would seem that, given that a certain basic minimum of repression and compulsion is still essential, they have not even reduced the socially customary kinds of repression to a minimum in their own society, but have rather replaced them by a repression of their own, of an even more horrific form:

It is like breaking in a horse. One person has to break it in, and then anyone can ride it. First of all, it's love or something like it, then afterwards it's only pleasure. The secret is terribly simple: you make a girl fall in love with you, sleep with her, and then after a time appear to be disappointed or lose interest. Then you leave her to the attention of the others, and it's done. She is a full member.[14]

Langhans announced: 'Life as it is led in the Commune has de-contracted sexual problems.' What is really meant is: 'As couples we had no success in de-contracting our sexuality so we tried the Commune.' The apparently uncompromising and

[14] From an article in a 1967 issue of the West German humorous weekly *Pardon*.

sexually revolutionary statements of the communards come close to resembling ostentatious pseudo-genitality – like the exhibitionist behaviour of the compulsively promiscuous American couples.[15] In this case the ostentation only seems explicable as the product of homosexual wishes – which (so far as we can tell) were significantly tabooed in the First Commune.

The First Commune wanted more. It wanted to destroy *the whole* of bourgeois culture, beginning 'here and now'. It shares this idea with the vast majority of the radicalized youth groups on the fringe. In these groups, this idea only materializes into force when it is a question of protesting against, and attempting to break down such 'bourgeois' qualities and character traits as fidelity, discipline, rational authority, even honesty. But the fact that the protest has not progressed beyond its personal anti-patriarchal character, directed against one's own family and standards, should not obscure the danger inherent in it, and in the loosening of standards: that this does make young people ever more incapable of resisting repressive desublimation. The bourgeois qualities mentioned above continue for the time being to be an essential condition for the development of sublimation and a strong ego, and the destruction of these qualities (even if, and indeed especially if, it takes place on the left) should not be confused with their supersession. The latter is one of the tasks of socialism; the former can only contribute to repressive desublimation.

The anti-bourgeois and anti-institutional attitude of the protest youth groups is a structural part of their political position, and without it they would immediately be absorbed or collapse. But in most individuals this attitude is still so fixated on the patriarchal family structure which caused it in the first place that it has something forced about it. This inner contradiction blocks the possibility of progress. For example, though it is necessary to fight the bureaucratic ossification and institutional mechanisms of integration in the power system, and to prevent their occurrence in one's own organization, it is extremely harmful to combat, individually and collectively, all forms of discipline within oneself and others as 'anal mechanisms', 'bureaucratic tendencies', etc., and replace them with a purely individual anti-anal principle. This has had devastating

[15] See for example Kunzelmann, in the issue of *Pardon* quoted: 'I have difficulties having orgasm, and I am glad to say this in print. Nothing could be more false than the bourgeois idea of entering once and for all into an exclusive relationship and stipulating that the only place in which it can finally be considered intolerable is in the grave.'

effects throughout the anti-institutional protest movement. Neurotic objections to work have been rationalized as a protest against being forced to learn; and badly organized demonstrations, badly stuck-on posters (which anyone can tear off), meetings announced too late in the day and inadequately prepared for, are recurrent phenomena in the anti-authoritarian groups.

Bourgeois culture is not just the ruling expression of manipulation and repression, it is also the summa of all socially achieved capacities for controlling nature, for thought, for the faculty of speech, for the purposeful use of mind and body. Although these faculties have always been fettered in bourgeois society, all the elements in our culture which have even proceeded so far towards liberation as to perceive that the fetters are there are today being systematically destroyed by the representatives of the culture itself. In materialist terms, repressive desublimation means going back on the cultural achievements of history, more especially sublimation. The Commune is but the most obvious expression of an unspoken tendency, which pervades the whole anti-authoritarian camp in the late capitalist countries, to join forces, from the other side of the fence, in destroying the achievements of civilization. Whereas the system manipulates culture out of existence, the protesters bulldoze it down. If the worst comes to the worst, the result will be that only the repressive aspects of civilization will remain, and the other aspects, the ones that are needed to build up a society that really would be capable of replacing the bourgeois order of things, will be destroyed.

The experience of these Communes – predominantly composed of students – permits one or two conclusions to be drawn.

For numerous young people, whether studying, working, or still at school, it is more politically meaningful, personally satisfying and liberating to form into communities, rather than to suffer the neurosis-producing atmosphere of student hostels, other kinds of hostels for single people, furnished rooms or the cramped environment of the parental home. In some circumstances they might find that self-run communities helped them to bear, *and* fight, the social and psychological pressure to which they are particularly susceptible as single people.

Every even remotely communal living arrangement among a set of people should start and continue on the assumption that it cannot be the task of the 'Commune' to solve all the personal and emotional problems of its members, and remedy the political weakness suffered by the opposition movement. On the other hand the Commune should be regarded as a functional unit, which can serve to increase the political capability of its members and make their mental existence easier.

All programmes such as the abolition of exclusive relationships, the establishment of flexible promiscuous groups, or relatively stable sexual relationships involving more than two people, integration of married couples or families into a larger communal context and so on cannot yet be systematically discussed, let alone successfully implemented. Where they do arise, it has to be spontaneous; anything in the nature of a programme must at all costs be avoided, since at the present moment it would always be to some extent unnatural, and thus repressive. It could not correspond to the psychological structure of the individuals, and so could not satisfy their needs. The average exclusive relationship, whether temporary or permanent, is less repressive, and above all less productive of neurosis, than compulsory promiscuity, even when the latter appears dressed in the clothes of liberation and the sexual revolution.

The only kind of Commune really conceivable today does not make any claims to abolish the family. It can be accounted a success if it simply accomplishes a thing which was one of the positive functions of the bourgeois family (though few today actually fulfil it): to provide protection against the hostile environment. It is senseless to break down the family even more when the system is breaking it down already. The usual result – as many recent Communes in West Germany have shown – is that the negative function of the contemporary family (inner terrorism) gets worse, and its classic positive function (protection against the outside world) stops.

There is also a temporal limit to the usefulness of the Commune. It serves its most positive function in the transition period from adolescent to adult life, during which it can take on a very important role in preventing the formation of neurosis and repressive desublimation. This temporal limitation may sound disagreeably repressive – to some degree it is repressive if measured against the ideal of an independent union of free people. But we are dealing with facts: how, in present circumstances we can combat the formation of neurosis and repressive desublimation. And people who want to take an active part in the class struggle require, like anyone else, a specific combination of psychological, interior development and external pressure. What this combination needs to be is determined, among other things, by their age.

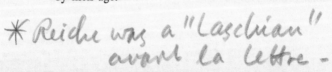

* Reiche was a "Laschian" avant la lettre -

One of the classic functions of the family is impossible, or very difficult, in the type of Commune outlined here: the upbringing of children. Brückner's statement that 'one cannot approach the socialization process in a spirit of dilettante experimentation' is of the utmost importance. No more satisfactory model for the early socialization of children exists in any of the highly developed capitalist industrial countries than averagely successful family upbringing (whether the success be the result of accident or design). The necessary conditions are: normal and loving parents, moderately favourable subsidiary factors such as secure economic circumstances, reasonable living conditions, satisfactory division of roles between the parents, and time for the mother to devote herself to the child. The progressive left are fond of quoting *Summerhill*[16] as an example of non-repressive communal education, but in fact it has a number of disadvantages as a model. Firstly, the children do not normally come to the boarding school in question before they are six; they come chiefly from those middle-class families in which relationships and techniques of upbringing have been above average in their rationality and freedom from repression. Secondly, the children are not in a commune of adults, but in a boarding school with adult personnel to look after them. Thirdly, the rate of psychosis-like breakdown in children leaving Summerhill appears to be significantly higher than in any comparable group of young people. The reason for this must be that young people at Summerhill have not learned to cope with the repressive institutions of society, and therefore have an extremely low degree of resistance to frustration – too low for our society. These young people have not learned some of the elementary faculties necessary for dealing with the outside world, whether by entering into a critical relationship with it or conforming to it, and because of their education, this outside world seems particularly threatening, hostile and repressive.

The preceding catalogue of necessary preconditions for and limitations of Communes in the present day does not deny the utopian aspect of Commune building, and its function as a precursor of things to come. But transformations are needed to allow this aspect to become a conscious one, and stop it either turning into an idealistic anachronism or changing into resignation or cynicism. The First Commune proclaimed as its foremost

16 A. S. Neill: *Summerhill: A Radical Approach to Education*, Penguin edn, Harmondsworth, 1968.

principle that the political practice of every individual member must always be directly related to the satisfaction of his needs. As Kunzelmann said, 'What do I care about the Vietnam war, if I have orgasm troubles?' We say, however, that the construction of a strong opposition to the Vietnam war in the cities of the late capitalist countries, and the reduction of orgasm troubles among the left-wing opposition in those cities have a joint precondition: the successful combating of neurosis formation and repressive desublimation. An orgasm is no more obtainable by trying than is a strong anti-Vietnam movement by quoting Lenin and Lukács. For the individual to attain any kind of personally satisfying success in both spheres, he needs a high degree of disciplined work *and* flexible spontaneity, of instinctual sublimation *and* liberation, of utopian idealism *and* trenchant realism.

## LOVE AND FIDELITY

Love and fidelity are typical bourgeois characteristics. The character-structure necessary to produce them has been described in previous chapters predominantly in terms of a complex ego-structure. This is a cultural phenomenon which can only arise when a highly complex system of social production is in operation; indeed, it is necessary for people's egos to be complex for them to be able to run such a system at all. In psychological terms, one can say that, phylogenetically, love and fidelity were brought fairly late into the sexual sphere. We have only fairly fragmentary knowledge of the love-life of the common mass of people before the end of the nineteenth century. It seems very likely, on socio-economic grounds, that it was even less 'human' than that of the upper classes then in power. The picture that has come down to us of the love-life of the upper classes of earlier historical periods seems to indicate that they behaved as adults in a way that only children do today – and at that only in their Oedipal and pre-Oedipal fantasies – casting out unlovable wives and mistresses, having rivals beheaded, banishing mistresses' husbands to lonely islands, having people they lusted after brought off the street into their bedrooms, etc. It took a thousand years for the religious-cum-civil law of monogamous and indissoluble marriage to become so internalized that it became a firm part of sexual morality. For this reason, from the early Middle Ages onwards, there were constantly recurring waves of stringent enforcement of chastity and morality, and of the most extreme sexual oppression. Normally these waves of strictness only applied either to specific groups within the ruling class (the top ranks of the clergy and the nobility), or else to the masses. They were generally put into effect with a quite unparalleled degree of terroristic cruelty. But in spite of this, they did not go very deep, as their short duration proves; they nearly always came to an end either after one generation or after the death of the ruler who had instigated them. This situation remained much the same until the capitalist social system came into being and radically changed it.

In pre-revolutionary France, under the rule of Louis XIV and Louis XV, the bourgeoisie had developed its own secure, though unyielding morality for sex and marriage *in opposition to* the ruling classes. This later became an important socio-psychological and political factor in its victory over feudalism. The bourgeoisie were more *moral*, and that implied, in the event, more healthy and disciplined, stronger and more honest, than the old regime. Love, marriage and sex were forged by the bourgeoisie into the quasi-natural triangle within whose iron bonds the family became the 'germ of the state' which it really was in the early and classic periods of capitalism. The specific oppression this inflicted on love, marriage and sexuality from the very beginning, and the specific way in which it maimed them, have been discussed in the second chapter of this book. But it was necessary, in order to put the new social system into force. And, with the same necessity, the bourgeoisie kept their distance, socially and juridically, from the utopian, revolutionary and social reform movements of the revolutionary and post-revolutionary period, which had made a radical critique of the institution of marriage and the ruling modes of love life. Their spokesmen got into the bourgeois salons but no further. Rousseau suffered this fate, as did later, Stendhal, Balzac and Georges Sand.

The repressive triangle of love, sexuality and marriage developed by the bourgeoisie was criticized in the Marxist-oriented psychoanalytic discussions of the pre-fascist period in pioneering depth, though inevitably no practical results emerged. Wilhelm Reich defined the social functions of marriage in three ways: economic, political and social:

*Economic*: Just as marriage, in human history, began to develop with the private ownership of the social means of production, so it continues to have its reason for existence in this economic basis. That is, as long as these economic conditions continue to exist, marriage is a social necessity. The objection that classes without such an economic interest live in the same form of sex life is erroneous, for the ruling ideologies are those of the ruling class; the form of marriage is based not only on economic factors, but also on the ideological moral atmosphere and on human structure. . . .

*Political*: Monogamous lifelong marriage is the nucleus of the compulsive family; this in turn . . . is the ideological training ground for every member of authoritarian society. In this lies the political significance and importance of marriage.

*Social*: The economic dependence of the woman and the children is a chief characteristic of patriarchal society. Secondarily, marriage thus becomes an economic and moral (in the sense of patriarchal interests) protection for women and children. Consequently, patriarchal and authoritarian society must of necessity uphold compulsive marriage.[17]

Reich thus also established that all proposals for marriage reform under capitalism are bound to contain a contradiction, however progressive their intention may be. However this same contradiction underlies his own model for the abolition of marriage: the 'lasting sexual relationship'. Reich believed that this was a model for a relationship capable of overcoming the sexually and politically harmful factors of compulsive marriage even before capitalism itself had been overcome. But he also proposed it as a model for regulating sexual, emotional and economic relationships in a free society. The most original, and yet at the same time problematic aspect of this model is that it is not just a collection of reformative or revolutionary advice, but a single system, which Reich called '*sex-economic self-regulation*'. This was a kind of cybernetic system of problem-solving covering the whole of social reality. The 'regulating' moment of this system was a 'libido cycle' liberated into full genitality. When genital sexuality was free to unfold to its full extent it would automatically cast off the bonds of the pregenital component instincts, and the destructive instincts would automatically lose the power to form themselves into aggression or hostility to sex, but could be harnessed without difficulty for socially useful activities. The person would be potent, 'capable of love' and 'sex-affirmative',[18] and as such have no difficulty in establishing long-lasting monogamous sexual relationships, because the compulsion to neurotic polygamy (Don Juanism) and the compulsion to equally neurotic monogamy (possessiveness, pre-Oedipal fixations, etc.) would have lost their basis. All that could then befall the 'lasting sexual relationship' would be that it would, after a while, probably become naturally 'dulled',[19] in

[17] *The Sexual Revolution*, pp. 131–2.   [18] op. cit., p. 15.
[19] op. cit., p. 122.

which case it could be dissolved with a minimum of violence, sense of loss, or fear.

The dualism of sexuality and destructiveness in the instinctual life, which preoccupied Freud to his life's end and later Herbert Marcuse, seemed to Reich a theoretical rather than a real problem. He considered that the freely developing libido contained within itself the means of stabilizing the personality and enabling the individual to cope successfully with reality. The drive to destruction could only become effective if the drive to sexuality was weak or hindered by fear. Any sexual morality, whether capitalist or socialist, would become superfluous: 'The principle of moral regulation is opposed to that of sex-economic self-regulation.'[20]

I have endeavoured to show, in a large number of differing examples, that the liberation of *genital* sexuality cannot be regarded as the decisive social and sexual revolutionary moment that Reich thought it to be. He certainly had greater historical justification for believing that the liberation of genital sexuality would lead to social liberation than have the progressive circles still holding this belief today. In his day genital sexuality was directly suppressed. But there are in his utopian construct of the 'lasting sexual relationship' elements of resignation, even re-action. It is founded on the principle that men and women are economically independent of each other, and would not be hindered in leaving each other, if they so desired, by *economic* factors. This is of course a necessary precondition for every free human relationship. But Reich assumed that in a sexual relationship attraction and pleasure mount for a while but then start to decrease, and seemed to believe that this rising and falling graph of sexual attraction was a law of nature. For instance, he writes:

Nobody would think of blaming anybody for not wanting to wear the same dress year in, year out, or for getting tired of eating the same food all the time. Only in the sexual realm has the exclusiveness of possession attained a great emotional significance.[21]

Reich suggests two ways of reacting to the 'dulling of sensual desire': permanent separation or temporary infidelity as a means of releasing sexual tension. In this he is in company of both the progressive marriage counsellors who came before Freud and the quasi-progressive and cynical marriage counsellors who came

---

[20] op. cit., p. 8.
[21] op. cit., p. 125.

after Kinsey. The sentence: 'In many cases, the cure for an un-happy marriage – moralists and authoritarian law not withstand-ing – is marital infidelity'[22] typifies this standpoint. Freud, precisely because he is so firmly fixed in the bourgeois view-point, has a more serious and conscientious perception of the case than Reich. For him, marital infidelity is only 'the cure for nervous illness arising from marriage',[23] the nervous tension itself being the neurotic expression of an ego that has been weakened by the high cultural demands placed upon it. This weakening is a cultural law, not a natural law. Freud was very careful not to say anything indicating that sexual tension was liable to decrease through quasi-natural causes. Reich was for-getting at this point that infidelity on the part of husband or wife would be bound to lead to jealousy, and that the situation could at best only go back to the *status quo*, which contained within itself the mechanisms producing the decrease of sexual tension. It is true that Reich said that a free sexual relationship was beyond the sphere of bourgeois fidelity and infidelity because the quality of the sexuality involved had rendered morally induced fidelity superfluous. But against this one must argue that no sexual relationship of whatever kind can be called free unless it is able to escape the sexual boredom which is now so frequent and familiar.

This boredom is in one sense the other side of the coin to neurotic jealousy. In contrast, jealousy does have, even where the person concerned has had a rational education, a legitimate basis in personal history. Jealousy, like the fear out of which it arises, is a reaction against a possible or a real loss of love. It is this fear, when it is properly used, that makes a child capable of higher, conscious and controlled love relationships. In this respect, the mechanism of infantile jealousy is a precondition for the development of the ego, but at the same time the ego, as it grows stronger, overcomes the infantile aspect of jealousy. Only the neurotic or psychotic person stays at, or regresses to, an infantile structure of jealous love. For this reason psycho-analysis distinguishes between competitive or normal jealousy on one hand, and projected and unreasonable jealousy on the other. The first form of jealousy is the natural reaction of a healthy person to possible or real loss of love, the second two are reaction-formations of a neurotic, or else a psychosis-like type.[24]

[22] op. cit., p. 144.
[23] *'Civilized' Sexual Morality and Modern Nervous Illness*, p. 195.
[24] See Freud: *Some Neurotic Mechanisms*, p. 223.

Reich stresses the social aspect of these reaction-formations, and consequently differentiates normal and possessive jealousy.

Analogously, he distinguishes between natural and neurotic boredom (the latter being Don Juanism). This distinction presents problems. When an ageing love relationship begins to get sexually unbearable, that is to say, when one partner reacts to the other with decreasing potency or total impotence, one would certainly discover, in analysing the particular situation, that the love relationship was entered into in the first place from a position containing elements, however small, of neurotic infatuation (or jealousy), and at least traces of infantile jealousy. That is why it is only in our *present* society that sexual boredom has as much justification as jealousy. Children have to be adapted in their upbringing to the competitive social norms. If they are to conform to these norms in later life, they have to be kept, in respect of jealousy, at an infantile level, and all the more so to the extent that such competitive norms are not justifiable by social reality. For this reason they have to revenge themselves on their parents through their treatment of every sexual object that comes into their 'possession'.

In our society, where everything is interchangeable with everything else, fidelity really does share the lot of the 'new dress'. The exchange-value of a dress decreases with its age, regardless of whether it has been worn or not. When people resist this compulsion, and continue to wear an article of clothing after it has gone out of fashion, they do it because they have become fond of it in the course of wearing it so long. It has become a part of them. This love is of different kind from the watered-down experience of an old marriage in which the partners only continue to have sexual relations with each other out of common memory; neither does it resemble the state of desire aroused by the fetishistic sexiness of the new dress seen in a shop window or walking down the street. Lasting love is equally proof against being dulled by time, or lured away by the sexiness of novelty. It holds fast to individual 'minimal differences' and resists the indiscriminate manipulated differentiation dictated, via fashion, by the compulsion that everything should be interchangeable. In a free society a sexual object would not be an object in the sense that one acquires and consumes clothes either out of expediency (work-clothes/wife) or for fetishistic reasons (fashions/transient affairs).[25]

---

[25] Significantly, the clothing that the young radical opposition most favours, and invests with the most sexual prestige, is the sort which bridges the gap

The same criticism can be applied to Reich's other suggestion for dealing with sexual boredom: permanent separation of the partners. Certainly it would be the best thing for both partners in a great many marriages and sexual relationships in existence today if they were to split up. But even in his model of the free and lasting sexual relationship, Reich was forced to give only evasive and euphemistic replies to the question, 'What happens to the partner whose love may persist?'[26] He gets tangled in 'realistic' considerations about weighing up which is the lesser of two evils. In fact it is this very model of the 'lasting sexual relationship' which makes most clear how compulsive and ultimately reactionary all utopias become when put into practical terms. The only categories available for describing the liberated state are those of coercion and dehumanization, and thus the liberating aspect itself becomes compromised.[27] Rightly, Wilhelm Reich points out that when boredom arises in a relationship, it cannot be restored 'by good intentions or by "love techniques" '.[28] But the internal logic of his model forces him to recommend 'infidelity' in what is virtually the capacity of a 'technique' for stabilizing a lasting sexual relationship. 'Numerous examples show,' he says, 'how clearly an occasional relationship with another partner only helped a relationship which was on the point of taking on the form of a compulsive marriage.'[29] Indeed, such cases exist in plenty. But what sort of a relationship can it be that benefits from a casual affair by one of the partners with someone else? Meanwhile the more recent marriage handbooks have taken over the principle of sex-economic self-regulation and turned it into a principle of total regulation from outside.

Theodor W. Adorno in his aphorism 'Constanze'[30] has said that the obligation to fidelity is one of bourgeois society's modes of

between working and fashionable clothes, and which, worn in this way, is a protest against the existence of the gap: jeans, leather jackets, army coats, etc.
[26] Reich: op. cit., p. 125.
[27] In fact, compared with other socialist sexual and educational utopias, Reich's seems the least susceptible to criticism on these grounds. The rest, as for example *Neues Kinderland* ('The Children's New World'), Basle, 1920, by a disciple of Adler's, Otto Rühle, read today like directions for bringing up children in the workhouse.
[28] Reich: op. cit., p. 124.
[29] op. cit., p. 125.
[30] Theodor W. Adorno: *Minima Moralia – Reflexionen aus dem beschädigten Leben* ('Reflexions from a damaged life'), Frankfurt, 1962, p. 226.

compulsion, but fidelity itself is an essential moment in resisting that society:

If love is to point the way to better things in society, it cannot do so by remaining in an idyllic corner; it has to come out as conscious resistance. But this demands a will to do something for its own sake, which the bourgeoisie, who are of course not satisfied with love as an end in itself, are bound to deny. Loving means not allowing the directness of one's own feelings to be interfered with by the ever present forces of mediation, of economy; fidelity mediates love to itself, and turns it into an obstinate force of resistance. A person can only be said to love if he has the strength to hold onto his love. Sublimated social interests have the power to condition sexual desire, and make now this, now that among the thousandfold objects sanctioned by the system appear spontaneously attractive. But where a person remains faithful to his original love, he is able to stand up to the gravitational pull of society, despite all the intrigues with which it is bound to try and capture him. The test of feeling is whether it can supersede feeling by constancy, even if it has to take the form of obsession. The person who is taken in by the lure of unreflective spontaneity, who proudly thinks of himself as honest in listening only to what he supposes is the voice of his heart, and in running away when he ceases to hear it, is, for all his sovereign independence, in fact the tool of society. Passive, without knowing it, all he does is accept whatever cards the interests of society deal to him. Love which betrays the beloved betrays itself. The obligation to fidelity imposed by society is the opposite of freedom, but it is only through fidelity that freedom can set up a rebellion against the dictates of society.

If a person demands fidelity of himself, as part of his individual programme against collective desublimation, it can impose an enormous strain on him. Whether this strain does violence to him – is repressive – whether in fact it is too high a price to pay for avoiding psychological regression, and is destructive in its effect, or whether the person has enough discipline at his command to cope successfully with it, must be determined for each individual case. The regressive compulsions inherent in the spontaneity which Adorno defined as illusory (infidelity, change of partner, etc.) cannot be avoided by personal endeavour. To describe this endeavour as 'holding onto one's love' is to hide its real nature, and talking about 'obsession' and 'rebellion' merely glorifies it. Will-power and subjective insight into the workings of repressive desublimation are not in themselves enough to make a person capable of getting rid of these compulsions once he has been attacked by them. The only possibility of success – and at that, only in a few fortunate individual cases – lies in the application of psychoanalytic techniques, or in a course of psycho-analysis.

It cannot therefore be the aim of this book to call for a new practical sexual morality for the left, or to give theoretical guidelines for the formation of such a morality. This would not only be an idle attempt. One would necessarily come to the wrong conclusions and demand the wrong courses of action if one were to start trying to decide, in present circumstances, whether in a free society people *ought* to live their sex lives as couples or in Communes, whether they should stay together for a while or for ever. The important thing at present is to take as much of the compulsion out of these relationships as possible. It is not marriage which has to be done away with but the *institution* of marriage; it is not love and jealousy which have to be done away with but the conditions producing mental and physical murder through jealousy, and mental and physical suicide through lack of love or injured love. The same is true of the legal position. What is needed is not an extension of the grounds for divorce or a humanization of family law, but the abolition of marriage and parental rights. In their place, only *children's rights* should be considered. In a free society marriage would not need protection, and there would not need to be any formal rules about who could live with them, at what age, or for how long. Individuals would be free to organize the private sphere as they wished, except for the upbringing of children. Ironically, this is almost the only sector of private life in which bourgeois society allows complete freedom. Whether it takes place in the Commune, or in a family of the traditional kind, the socialization process of early childhood will always be of absolutely central importance to society. This means that it cannot be left unconditionally to the love, inclinations and weaknesses of single members, or groups of members, of the adult population.

Today we cannot help but think in certain concepts, and make certain distinctions – for instance the distinction between those who are growing up and those who are grown up – which may, in a free society, become partially or wholly out of date. Even if we want to anticipate the future by bringing even a few of the basic social processes into the form needed for a free society – as, for example, a non-repressive system of upbringing which would produce adults with strong egos and the faculty for happiness – we have still to labour under the disadvantage of only having concepts and modes of thought at our disposal which refer to processes in the *existing* society. This is what makes it so difficult to outline models of human communication, education, use of natural resources, etc., with a built-in maximum of freedom and minimum of repression, and which are neither excessively vague and abstract, nor simply a negation of existing social conditions and mechanisms (anti-authoritarian, non-repressive, non-alienating work, etc.). In interpreting recent student revolts in West Germany and West Berlin, Herbert Marcuse talked about 'the end of Utopia': 'The new possibilities for a humane society and its environment cannot be conceived as a continuation of the old, cannot even be set in the same historical continuum as the old. The new possibilities presuppose 'a break in the historical continuum'. Marcuse went on to say that 'all the material and intellectual forces needed for the realization of a free society are there.'[31] In terms of the new revolutionary anthropology, which it is our task to develop, this means that the highly industrialized countries of today are ripe enough for a revolution extending beyond the reorganization of the forces of production. Development and refinement is needed within the human psyche to correspond to the level already reached in man's power over nature, and to guarantee its continuation. This power will in turn be extended to developments of a biological kind. These developments demand changes in organization and changes in the content of human life which are qualitatively different from current forms in present-day highly industrialized countries, whether capitalist or socialist.

When we are considering the *practical* problems of the revolutionary reorganization of human life, such as the upbringing of children, the sublimation and channelling of the instincts in childhood and adolescence, the form and content of living together, of sexuality, etc., – and what else are they but practical problems? – we have to be strong enough to continuously face up to one factor which makes the necessary 'break' very difficult. We possess the material and intellectual means for constructing a free society – but our entire intellectual capacity, when we turn it to criticism, is related only to existing societies. Though therefore it may be true that the qualitative difference between the existing and a free society can only be established through a 'break in the historical continuum', it is equally true, firstly, that this break can only be theorized about in advance in categories, modes of thought and dreams bearing the hallmark of the existing society, and the oppression, exploitation and deprivation of liberty practised in it. Secondly, that it will have to be carried out by people who, though they suffer under this

[31] Herbert Marcuse: *Das Ende der Utopie*, Berlin, 1967, pp. 11 and 14.

oppression, exploitation and deprivation of liberty, recognize them for what they are, and want to do away with them, are also marked, and maimed by them, in their most minute feelings and habits. And thirdly, that the free society can only be built up on the basis of the maimed and fettered capacities of unfree societies. Otherwise it would be meaningless to say that we already have the intellectual forces necessary for the realization of a free society.

This completes the sketch of the 'new anthropology' which is our task for the future. It will be negative – and revolutionary.

# Postscript 1970

Certain comrades have levelled some basic criticisms at this book. I will deal successively with the following points raised, without attempting a systematic refutation: Marxist versus positivist terminology; failure to take account of the realm of production; projection of the psychological structure of middle-class youth onto the whole working-class; love and fidelity; homosexuality; transfer of psychoanalytic concepts to historical development.

The permanent fluctuation between Marxist and empirical sociological terminology in *Sexuality and Class Struggle* is necessary in so far as it marks one of the shortcomings of our class analysis. According to the precise Marxist concepts it is not difficult to say who from the 'middle classes' or the 'petty-bourgeoisie' are in fact wage labourers; it can be established by their position in the productive process (whether productive or unproductive workers). Also the problem as to which part of the intelligentsia belongs to the 'collective worker' (Marx) is not insoluble: namely, that part whose work is immediately employed in the production of surplus value. However, categorizing all those formerly described as middle class as proletariat brings clarity only on paper. For the concept of the proletariat also has a directly political aspect, which, in answering the question why certain groups engage in struggle (become class-conscious), is related to superstructural or socio-psychological problems. Hence, when such problems were under discussion, I chose to counterpose middle class and lower class in order to be able to describe the differences still existing in upbringing, inherited ideology, the collective dimensions of needs, etc. These differences and the variations in the formation of class consciousness deriving from them become obscured if one simply speaks, at this level, of the 'proletariat'.

The same is true for the conceptual heterogeneity in my description and analysis of 'cultural' phenomena. I have sometimes spoken of late capitalism, sometimes of cultural level, sometimes of imperialism. Perhaps this makes for ambiguity in some places, or even error. Basically however this heterogeneity is unavoidable. For there is no 'Marxist terminology' for psychological processes, even for collective ones. And quite rightly so. There is in general no rigid Marxist terminology. Our task is rather to clarify in materialist fashion mental processes and their cultural effects.

More pertinent is a criticism that forms the rational kernel of the above. The accusation has been made that my investigation, exactly where it aspires to take account of the interaction between the collective organization of the instincts and the reproduction of specifically capitalist production relations, is still restricted to the realm of consumption or, at best, to that of the realization of surplus value, and nowhere deals with the creation of surplus value (the realm of production) itself. Now it is a central thesis of *Sexuality and Class Struggle* that the ever-present problems of overproduction make it necessary to relax the classic obsessional anal character. This thesis however cannot directly be deduced from the relations of production alone. For in the realm of production what still counts, with only a few exceptions, are exactly the old 'anal' laws of order, thrift and rigid sexual morality. In order to discover the 'relaxation' in the character structure, in order to exhibit the new cultural forms of instinct combination and transformation, and the integration of instinct and consciousness, one must necessarily analyse the realm of consumption, unless one has access to clinical interviews. The decisive faults in my analysis do not arise from the fact that I concentrated on the realm of consumption, but rather from the *way* I treated it.

My analysis consequently can easily give the impressions that for example, the classic 'anal character' is not only 'relaxed' but has disappeared altogether. This is certainly not the case. The collective tendencies towards 'perpetual puberty' are, in the first place, certainly not equally strongly established for all social strata, and secondly are quite conceivable in a form of integration with very strong anal reaction-formations. The central point is that, because production and consumption at present induce such contrary models of behaviour, something like a collective tendency towards ego-division arises: individuals must cultivate two contradictory character traits, and daily demonstrate the corresponding modes of behaviour – rigidity, classic authoritarianism and anti-sexuality at work; 'relaxation', objectless fetishism and 'apparent sexuality' in free time.

Another criticism attacks the same weakness. I have very often projected the psychological processes of middle-class youth onto the whole working class. This is especially evident in the discussions of latent homosexuality, fashion and the dissolution of strong sexual roles. That this projection is a direct result of the anti-authoritarian theoretical formation is shown in the Preface to this edition.

*Sexuality and Class Struggle* is naturally also a book on revolutionary morality. It should thus have an ego-supporting or even pedagogic function for the schools' movement, although this was not my intention at the time. Unfortunately, this morality is presented on some crucial issues in a very moralistic way. This reproach is made especially with respect to the treatment of 'love and fidelity' and of homosexuality. What hits hardest is the charge by some comrades that *Sexuality and Class Struggle* itself is repressive as the result of the way in which it calls for 'love and fidelity':

Recommendations of love and fidelity appear to cater to a widespread need. They express a straightforward protective function. Radical criticism of the suppression of sexuality makes radical demands on the individual which he does not feel able to live up to. The more conceivable general free sexuality becomes, the more the internal and external oppositions to its practice are experienced as insurmountable, while real sexual life loses as much pleasure as internal legitimacy. The result is often not greater freedom, but greater pressure. This condition causes illness. It would seem that Reiche's book, in this context, will be used by many as an excuse. He who inherits a belief in the high value of fidelity has an easier job to restabilize his behaviour.[1]

In fact, at big public meetings and in private discussion, I was very disturbed to find people quoting my book, of all things, to justify their messed-up marriages, to support terroristic relationships, or to give themselves a final repressive thrust towards adopting an 'obsessional socialist character'. This critique gained in importance in so far as I myself found the call to 'love and fidelity' highly repressive, and questionable even from the standpoint of orthodox psycho-analysis. I particularly proposed it as a *defence technique* against repressive desublimation. In the critique quoted it is said correctly:

Reiche demands conformity to the ideal of love and fidelity and thus intends to build up an opposition to the social trend of dissociating sexuality as a means of satisfaction from its connexion with this ideal. There would be nothing to object to in this if love were based on the

[1] Wolfgang F. Haug: 'Sexuelle Verschwörung des Spätkapitalismus?' ('The Sexual Conspiracy of Late Capitalism?') in *Neue Kritik*, no. 51/52, 1969, p. 101.

loved one and fidelity on love. But here love and fidelity are brought in as defence techniques. These ideals thus take on, in Reiche's book, a doctrinaire character.[2]

Similarly, Erich Wulff accuses *Sexuality and Class Struggle* of 'characteristically upholding the taboo on homosexuality', it being conclusively demonstrable 'that the abolition of this taboo brings about a liberation'.[3] The first part of this criticism is nonsense, the second highly questionable. In the first place I naturally did not take up a position against homosexuality in general but against the form in which homosexuality is customarily found in our society, namely against the *obsessive condition*, against compulsive fixation on the same sex. In its proper sexual political content the book is even rather the contrary, a polemic against *obsessive heterosexuality*.

In the second part of this criticism a more general reproof is put forward, which Wulff formulated as follows: 'Does not the flight into the distant future of absolute sexual freedom express the fear of the next step of liberation?' The principle behind this criticism is roughly this: the most progressive bourgeois sexual enlightenment (as represented in a majority of the illustrated papers) has a system-stabilizing, adaptive, but also a latent explosive, function. The stabilizing side is represented by the attempt to neutralize sexual conflicts and consequently to gloss over their social origins. The latent explosive side of this process is expanded by Haug with respect to fashion, etc., as follows:

'Pseudo satisfaction' however is also to be understood differently: it signifies firstly apparent, superficial satisfaction, secondly satisfaction that attempts to escape from the realm of mere appearance and become reality. It is not a condition that can be stabilized. This explains the general increase of frustration noted by Reiche. In the sphere of clothing and fashion some sort of symbolic licence can be bought that dissolves or circumvents formerly admissible norms of the canalizations of sexuality. By 'symbolic' we mean that modes of sexual behaviour formerly impossible are made possible in the form of appearance alone; in the general exterior display, sexuality proper remains temporarily suspended. This process can be seen as the beginning of a collective ego-amplification: the state of desiring and expressing something vaguely which one is not yet able to realize. Many people for example advertise themselves as 'general sexual' beings and are nevertheless tied in their still unchanged behaviour to conjugality.

[2] Haug: op. cit., p. 100.
[3] Eric Wulff: review of *Sexualität und Klassenkampf* in *Das Argument*, no. 56, 1970, p. 83.

Others advertise themselves as homosexual objects without being able to accept the physical approaches of their own sex. Superficially many of the system's collective inhibitions are annulled, though in reality they are still in force, institutionally as well as individually. Reiche notices the resulting tension, but he declares it to be a repressive swindle, although it is only repressive in the sense of being relaxed. However, what he takes for the last glimmers of the setting sun could equally turn out to be the first rays of freedom.[4]

Haug is certainly right here in so far as he indicates a historical tendency towards a change of sexual behaviour, taboos and sexual character. But the belief that this change makes the adaptation of individuals to the capitalist system less sure, or even endangers capitalist relations, is quite false. I am convinced that the condition Haug describes can and already does have a stabilizing function. A whole number of empirical signs bear this out. For example, many of us not so long ago were interpreting the enjoyment and the massive extension in the use of marijuana as just such a significant symbol of liberation which would spread from appearance to reality, so that the drug-induced phantasies themselves seemed to strain towards their own realization. The opposite however has occurred: the 'new' world of appearance has, in the USA just as in England and West Germany, tended to stabilize the old reality. This holds especially for those social groups that we used to term 'ripe for protest': the school students and other middle-class youth. A corresponding tendency is plainly visible in the results of the 'new' sexual enlightenment in West German schools. From intensive interviews with pupils (especially in the 14–16 age range) a regular pattern emerges. On the one hand sexual enlightenment and the ability to speak openly about sexual matters that would have been inconceivable in West Germany even two years ago, coupled with intense sexual activity carried on without the parents' knowledge and without the slightest guilt-feelings; on the other hand, however, an extremely conflict-free adaptation to current social norms, including specifically sexual norms, as established for young people in the last two years by the major agencies of manipulation. These pupils exhibit a similar blindness towards all contemporary and visible social conflicts and sexual ideologies, a blindness which is at best no less than that of three or four years ago.

I am naturally as little opposed to the superficial symbolization of sexual freedom as I am to marijuana, homosexuality, or

---

[4] Haug: op. cit., p. 105.

adultery. The question is only how to evaluate these phenomena strategically. I would like to discuss this problem again with the particular example of homosexuality.

We should firstly not imagine that the burden of sexual enlightenment and the formulation of new modes of sexual integration lies on our shoulders alone. Sexual enlightenment and the prefiguration of 'new' modes of sexual integration is also a department within the indigenous socialization of individuals into capitalist society. Thus one can point to something like a 'natural law' of the relaxation and partial destruction of sexual taboos and old forms of sexual repression and behaviour. The end of the taboo on homosexuality is itself an instance of this 'law'. It takes place naturally and was begun independently of us. We should not act as if we were the only ones who campaigned for the abolition of the *social* taboo on homosexuality. Our task is rather that of intervening in this objective process so that it works against the adaptation of individuals to capitalism.

It is for example correct that 'exclusive' or obsessive homosexuality would be much more frequently encountered as an ego-symptom if it were not socially proscribed. This ego-symptom adjustment is naturally a basic and essential step towards the supersession of all socially over-fulfilled and compulsively maintained sexual role identities, certainly including heterosexual ones. Many of the mechanisms through which the behaviour of homosexuals today acquires a 'pathological' character would also become superfluous, and there would be a relaxation of the pressure that weighs on 'obsessive' heterosexuals, and forces them to display their unimpeded 'masculine' or 'feminine' qualities in a repressive way. For a supersession of the *social* taboo on homosexuality is certainly not conceivable without a corresponding transformation of heterosexual norms. And yet a control within this transformation is conceivable – and already visible – towards which one should be extremely sceptical. I have attempted to describe this control as the 'genital façade' and the 'incapacity for object-choice'. The corresponding personality-type is epitomized by the 'modern homosexual', already signalled by the most sophisticated tendencies in the mass media. Our 'propagation' of homosexuality must thus always include a criticism of homosexuality, just as our 'propaganda' for specific heterosexual models of behaviour includes a principled criticism of exclusive heterosexuality.

Haug's last criticism also conceals an inhibited attitude toward the elaboration of the 'sexual character' which will arise from the supersession of the bourgeois sexual character. Before I take a position on this, I must first mention a fundamental self-criticism which is necessary to the understanding of what follows. My book suffers from an in-built ambivalence: on the one hand critique of the bourgeois sexual character, on the other an idealized stylization of the *genital character*, as Wilhelm Reich calls it, or *genital primacy* as it is generally known in orthodox psycho-analysis.

*Genital primacy* lies behind all discussions in the book as *the* unspoken norm of cultural aspiration. An extremely *reformist* demand is concealed in this: namely the liberation of sexuality and character structure from pre-Oedipal and especially from anal entanglements in which it remains fettered by the specifically bourgeois form of the dissolution of the Oedipus complex. To a certain extent I was concerned merely to see genital primacy *really* established. This demand is however restrictive as it remains tied both to the level of development of human relations attained or intended by bourgeois society and to the collective vicissitudes of the instincts corresponding to this. The opposite *revolutionary* demand would be: liberation of sexuality from its *genital* fetters too. When I expressed this self-criticism in discussion I was accused of making a 'utopia of a post-genital culture' and of a false 'transfer of psychoanalytic categories onto history and sociology'.[5] I have certainly made some cautious attempts to apply the psychoanalytic model of specific phases of sexual, emotional and personality development to the development of collectivities (or social stages). In this I have kept closely to the writings of Freud and other psychoanalytical authors, such as Parin and Morgenthaler, on the theory of civilization. What I wished to guard against is expressed in the works, so outstanding in their psychoanalytic narrow-mindedness, of Anne Parsons[6] and Charles N. Sarlin,[7] at that time unknown to me.

Perhaps it is going too far to speak, as I did on the basis of certain psychoanalysts working in ethnology, of 'anal' or 'oral' cultures. It can be nevertheless empirically demonstrated that

[5] This accusation, as frequent among us as it is limited, is partially accounted for by the anti-ethnological bias of the entire German left. Since Friedrich Engels there has been only one serious attempt in Germany to evaluate the results of ethnology for a Marxist theory of culture, that of W. Reich in his discussion of Malinowski.

[6] Anne Parsons: 'Is the Oedipus Complex Universal?' in Munsterberger and Axelrod (eds.): *The Psychoanalytical Study of Society*, vol. III, New York, 1964.

[7] C. N. Sarlin: 'Identity, Culture and Psychosexual Development' in *American Imago*, XXIV, 1967.

the progression of individual socialization through specific stages, as psycho-analysis has elaborated it, also has a collective and historical dimension: individuals of entire social (or cultural) stages remain fixed in passive oral dependence, in anal reaction-formation, in phallic rivalry or in the dissolution of the Oedipus complex in such a way that they are unable to accomplish results, or to think in categories which we acquired at the anal phase. To all these different *collective* results of the socialization of libidinal and aggressive impulses correspond various reality principles. These different reality principles are thus only psychoanalytical concepts for the characterization of the levels of development attained at various times in the interchange of man and nature and in the resulting *formation of needs*. If this idea is correct, then one can also, from the development of collective and individual structures of need and satisfaction and the character structures corresponding to them, reason beyond genital primacy, at least in the negative sense. (This is what I meant by the 'revolutionary negative anthropology' of which there is such obscure talk at the end of *Sexuality and Class Struggle*.) In other words 'post-genital cultures' are conceivable and realizable, or at least levels of the development of needs at which the sexuality of developed man will no longer be distinguished according to whether they are polymorphous-perverse or genital, but according to quite different categories and gradations of the libidinal and aggressive impulses, which lie beyond this distinction and of which we can have no clear conception. We are not able to conceive of these new categories and gradations because our thought only functions with 'genital' categories with a strong 'anal' emphasis: such categories as domination, subjugation, and adaptation, the unlimited repetitive curve of tension and satisfaction, categories of separation and unification under pain and pleasure. We are certainly not in a position to conceive pleasure without pain or satisfaction without tension. 'The completely developed individual' of whom Marx speaks can in no way be the individual of 'genital primacy'. 'Genital primacy' marks only a stage, if so far the most developed one, in the history of the species – the formation of mankind.

The style of *Sexuality and Class Struggle* has been repeatedly criticized as in-group jargon, especially as it appeared that the book satisfied a general need and was read and discussed outside the narrow circle of our movement. I only hope that the English translation is clearer than the sometimes rather stilted and pedantic German original.

Perhaps English and American readers will be disappointed that in this postscript the questions of practical sexual politics (and sexual education) remain as open as in the book itself. They may also be disappointed that I have not in any way concerned myself with the differences between German capitalism and that of other countries. However, I think the latter is really the task of English readers and that the former cannot be my personal task. I only hope that *Sexuality and Class Struggle*, even where it stresses the German variants in collective organization under capitalism and where it is a product of our own political movement, is still sufficiently lucid for English and American comrades to relate these problems to their own political work.

*Long live victory in the class struggle!*